You Turn to Fitness

Jason Conviser, Ph.D., FACSM

Jenny Conviser, Psy.D.

Greg Ewert, MD

ISBN: 1-58518-931-6
Library of Congress Control Number: 2005922996
Book layout: Jeanne Hamilton
Book cover: Jennifer Stahlberger and Jeanne Hamilton

The authors wish to thank Technogym USA for their permission to reprint photos found throughout this book.

Healthy Learning
P.O. Box 1828
Monterey, CA 93942
www.healthylearning.com

Dedication

To all those who make the commitment to regain control of their lives through exercise, diet, and daily physical activity. You have made the ultimate You Turn!

Preface

What do cardiovascular disease, hypertension, stroke, high cholesterol, certain cancers, diabetes, obesity, arthritis, osteoporosis and various psychological disorders have in common? Within each of these chronic diseases or disorders, exercise plays a significant role in their prevention, treatment or control.

You may not realize that exercise is the BEST MEDICINE available today and probably the closest thing to the Fountain of Youth. Exercise adds years to your life as well as life to your years. At You Turn, we believe that EVERYONE should "fulfill an exercise prescription" and participate in an exercise program because youth and feeling youthful is at your finger tips.

The business of You Turn is health improvement. Our method of improving health is through exercise and adopting a healthy lifestyle. We provide compassionate, non-intimidating "health clubs" for the real America versus the one that bombards our television screens. We welcome people with real health issues (out of shape, overweight, chronic physical conditions, high blood pressure, etc.). We're so confident in the benefits of exercise that we provide a 100% money-back guarantee to our patrons who "fulfill their exercise prescription". We stand behind our belief by guaranteeing improvements like lowered body fat, reduced blood pressure and cholesterol as well as increased strength, endurance, and flexibility.

Whether you join a You Turn facility or not, it is our intent to spread the word on exercise. We hope that **You Turn to Fitness** provides its readers, especially beginner exercisers, with information concerning the how and why to exercise as well as how they can make informed and safe choices regarding their health.

Todd Dickson, President
You Turn

You Turn Health & Fitness
1000 Butterfield Rd., Suite 1007
Vernon Hills, IL 60061
(847) 968 – 5511 Phone
(847) 968 – 5512 Fax
www.youturnhealth.com

Contents

CHAPTER ONE

EXERCISE IS MEDICINE

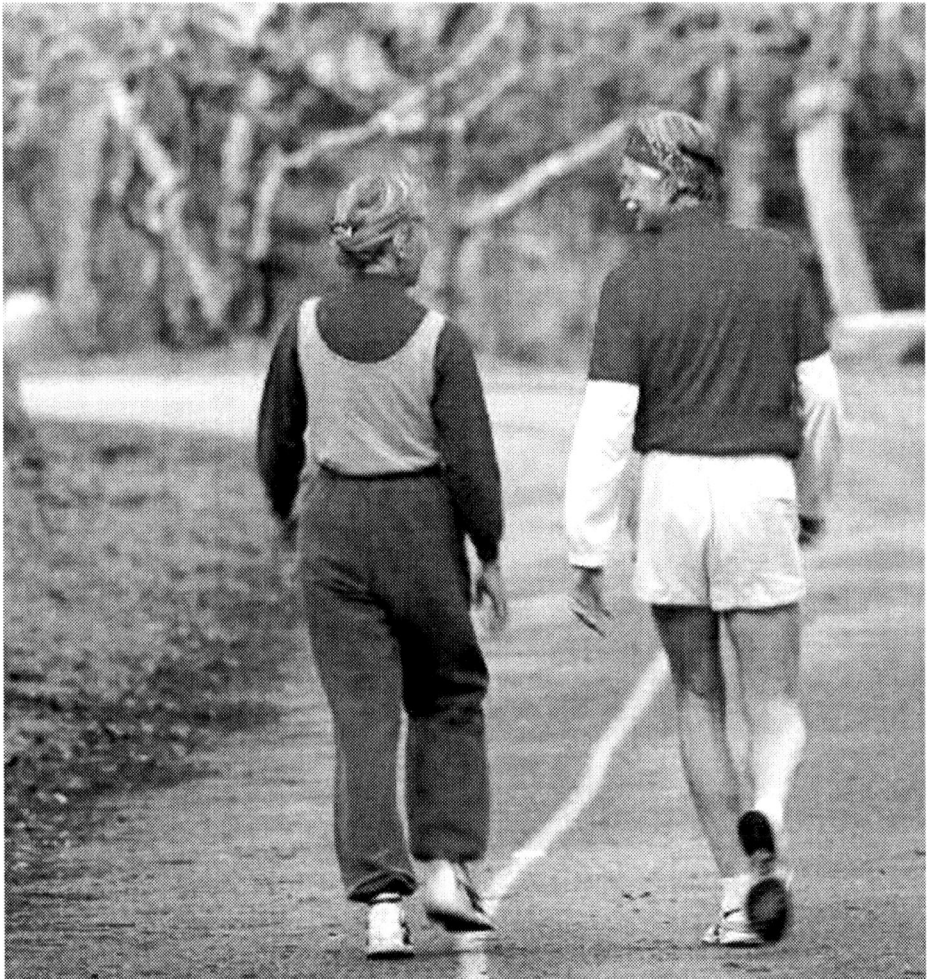

There is overwhelming evidence that exercise has substantial medical benefits for individuals of all ages.

Americans spend more than 1.5 trillion dollars annually for health care. This meteoric figure translates into an expenditure of over $5,500 for every man, woman and child in the United States. Another way of looking at this is that 16¢ of every single dollar spent in America is spent on health care. Regrettably, this financial commitment has neither shown signs of abating, nor produced meaningful results with regard to treating a wide variety of chronic health problems.

Attempts to identify the factors that have been major contributors to this virtual epidemic of medical problems have produced an array of probable reasons why such a large number of individuals are so apparently unhealthy…poor eating habits, a sedentary lifestyle, stress, smoking etc. At the same time, a number of attempts have been undertaken to identify what—if anything—can be done to diminish either the number or the severity of the medical problems affecting the public. These efforts have provided considerable evidence that exercise has substantial medicinal benefits for individuals of all ages.

Two of the most widely publicized efforts to investigate the possible relationship between exercise and disease were longitudinal studies, each of which involved more than 10,000 individuals. Several years ago, in a renowned study of Harvard graduates, Ralph Paffenbarger, M.D., found that men who expended approximately 300 calories a day—the equivalent of walking briskly for 45 minutes—reduced their death rates from all causes by an extraordinary 28%. A more recent study conducted by Dr. Steven Blair, of the Institute of Aerobics Research in Dallas documented the fact that a relatively modest amount of exercise has a significant effect on the mortality rate of both men and women. The higher the fitness level, the lower the death rate (after the data was adjusted for age differences between subjects in this eight-year investigation of 13,344 individuals). In addition, Blair and his group discovered that even if you are not initially fit and begin participation in an exercise program, you too can decrease your risk of premature death by up to 50 percent compared to those who don't exercise. An analysis of the extensive data yielded by both studies suggests one inescapable conclusion—EXERCISE IS MEDICINE.

Accepting the premise that regular exercise can play a key role in reducing your risk of incurring a medical problem and in decreasing your ultimate costs for health care is crucial. Despite the vast number of individuals who lead a sedentary lifestyle, the need for and the value of exercising on a regular basis is an irrefutable fact of life (and death). For example, Paffenbarger concluded after a detailed review of the results of his long-term investigation that **not exercising had the equivalent impact on your health of smoking one and one-half packs of cigarettes a day**. Fortunately, with few exceptions, most people are too sensible to ever consider ravaging their health by smoking excessively. Unfortunately, many of these same people fail to recognize the extraordinary benefits of exercise in preventing and treating medical problems.

You Turn Health & Fitness
1000 Butterfield Rd., Suite 1007
Vernon Hills, IL 60061
(847) 968 – 5511 Phone
(847) 968 – 5512 Fax
www.youturnhealth.com

YOU
TURN

HEALTH & FITNESS

Exercise R$_X$

Patient: _____

- ☐ Cardiovascular
  - ○ Frequency: _____ Days/Week
  - ○ Intensity: _____ Target Heart Rate
  - ○ Time: _____ Minutes
  - ○ Restrictions:_____
- ☐ Muscular Strength/Endurance
  - ○ Frequency: _____ Days/Week
  - ○ Restrictions:_____
- ☐ Flexibility
  - ○ Frequency: _____ Days/Week
  - ○ Restrictions:_____

Special Instructions:

Physician Signature: _____   Date: _____

*Unless specified, all exercise prescriptions will follow guidelines established by the American College of Sports Medicine.

Figure 1-1. Imagine a healthcare system where exercise is prescribed by physicians

The You Turn Prescription—Take 10 Exercises and Call Me In the Morning

As recently as 2004, the Centers for Disease Control reported that the number two cause of death among adults is cardiovascular disease (cancer of all types still being number one). In numerous studies over the past ten years, researchers have unequivocally demonstrated the relationship between levels of fitness and reduced risk of developing cardiovascular disease and chronic disease of all types. This means if you exercise you have a significantly reduced risk of dying prematurely from a heart attack, especially in your young adult years. Any listing of the medical problems and health-related conditions that can be at least partially treated and controlled by exercise would be extensive. Among the most significant of these health concerns and the manner in which exercise is thought to help alleviate each condition are the following:

- **Allergies**. Exercise is one of your body's most efficient ways to control nasal congestion and the accompanying discomfort of restricted nasal blood flow.

- **Angina**. Regular aerobic exercise dilates your vessels, increasing blood flow—thereby improving your body's ability to extract oxygen from the bloodstream.

- **Anxiety**. Exercise triggers the release of mood-altering chemicals in your brain.

- **Arthritis**. By forcing a skeletal joint to move, exercise induces the manufacture of synovial fluid and helps to distribute it over your cartilage and to force it to circulate throughout the joint space.

- **Back Pain**. Exercise helps to both strengthen your abdominal muscles and your lower back extensor muscles and stretch your hamstring muscles.

- **Bursitis and Tendonitis**. Exercise can strengthen your tendons—enabling them to handle greater loads without being injured.

- **Cancer**. Exercise helps you maintain your ideal body weight and helps keep your level of body fat to a minimum.

- **Carpal Tunnel Syndrome**. Exercise helps build up the muscles in your wrists and forearms—thereby reducing the stress on your arms, elbows, and hands.

- **Cholesterol**. Exercise will raise your level of HDL (the "good" cholesterol) in the blood and help lower your level of LDL (the "bad" cholesterol).

- **Diabetes**. Exercise helps lower excess blood sugar levels, strengthen your muscles and heart, improve your circulation, and reduce stress.

- **Fatigue**. Exercise can help alleviate the fatigue-causing effects of stress, poor circulation and blood oxygenation, bad posture, and poor breathing habits.

- **Headaches**. Exercise helps force your brain to secrete more of the body's opiate-like, pain-dampening chemicals (e.g., endorphins and enkephalins).

- **Heart Disease**. Exercise helps promote many changes that collectively lower your risk of heart disease—a decrease in body fat, a decrease in LDL, an increase in the efficiency of the heart and lungs, a decrease in blood pressure, and a lowered heart rate.

- **High Blood Pressure**. Exercise reduces the level of stress-related chemicals in your bloodstream that constrict arteries and veins, increases the release of endorphins, raises the level of HDL in your bloodstream, lowers your resting heart rate (over time), improves the responsiveness of your blood vessels (over time), and helps reduce your blood pressure by keeping your leaner.

- **Insomnia**. Exercise helps reduce your level of muscular tension and stress.

- **Intermittent Claudication**. Exercise helps improve peripheral circulation.

- **Knee Problems**. Exercise helps strengthen the structures attendant to the knee—muscles, tendons, and ligaments—thereby facilitating the ability of your knee to withstand stress.

- **Lung Disease**. Exercise helps strengthen the muscles associated with breathing and helps boost the oxygen level in your blood.

- **Memory Problems**. Exercise helps to improve your cognitive ability by increasing the blood and oxygen flow to your brain.

- **Menstrual Problems and Pre-Menstrual Syndrome**. Exercise helps to control the hormonal imbalances often associated with PMS by increasing the release of beta-endorphins.

- **Osteoporosis**. Exercise promotes bone density—thereby lowering your risk of suffering a bone fracture.

- **Overweight and Obesity Problems**. Exercise suppresses your appetite, increases your metabolic rate, burns fat, increases lean muscle mass, and improves your level of self-esteem.

- **Varicose Veins**. Exercise can help control the level of discomfort caused by existing varicose veins and help you prevent getting any additional varicose veins.

MORE EXERCISE, LESS DRUGS

An increasing amount of evidence suggests that spending more money on health care cannot and will not produce the financial benefits that could be achieved if every

American adopted better health practices—particularly a physically active lifestyle. A recent article in the New England Journal of Medicine commented on the results of the Nurses Health Study, estimated that in the past three decades, a number of efforts have documented the fact that regular physical activity can enable you to live both better and longer. And yet, several chronic health problems and conditions exist that are still treated almost solely with conventional medical therapy.

The point to remember is that exercise can be an extremely effective way to help treat a diverse array of chronic medical problems. As a result, properly prescribed exercise can lower your health care costs, not only by reducing the incidence or severity of your health problems in many cases, but also, when you do become ill, by diminishing your reliance on drugs and your need to expend your resources.

Are the positive consequences that result from exercising regularly worth the required effort? Absolutely! Should you make exercise an integral part of your daily regimen? Of course, you should. In countless ways, your life may depend on it.

CHAPTER TWO

MAKING A COMMITMENT
TO TOTAL FITNESS

Are the benefits of regular exercise worth the time and the effort? Absolutely!

Deciding whether to start a program of regular exercise is a straightforward decision if you are interested in your health, well being, and appearance. The answers to some simple questions show how easy your decision should be. Are the benefits of regular exercise worth the time and effort involved? Without question! Can an exercise program be designed that is appropriate to your particular interests and needs? Absolutely! How soon will you see results? No quick answer to this one. Some bodies respond more quickly than others. At You Turn, our strategy is to design an individualized program, monitor your progress on a daily basis, modify the program to meet your individual needs and let the body adapt to the exercise the way it has been designed for millions of years.

Everyone has seen before-and-after pictures of men and women who turned fat or skinny bodies into healthy, muscular figures. No such changes happen overnight like many advertisers want you to believe, and they aren't accomplished merely by thinking, wishing, or even by prayer. They require that you commit to a lifestyle of sound choices regarding your health.

The point to keep in mind is that even small steps can collectively have a major impact on your health. Although incremental acts, such as walking during your lunch hour, eating a piece of fruit instead of a candy bar, playing with your kids, etc., can seem inconsequential, eventually they do make a difference. Accordingly, the sooner you get started on an exercise program, the sooner you will experience the countless benefits of exercising.

A Little Exercise Can and Does Go a Long Way

Regular exercise has a positive effect on both the length and the quality of your life. In other words, exercising can enable you not only to live longer but live better. The impact of sound exercise on your health and sense of well being is substantial and well documented. For example, exercise can improve your ability to perform activities of daily living, make you think more clearly, improve your ability to maintain your weight at the desired level, improve your mood, and even have a positive impact on your sex life. More importantly, exercise can substantially reduce your risk of contracting certain diseases and medical conditions, all caused by or conditions worsened by being physically inactive. Dr. Larry Gibbons, medical director of the Institute of Aerobics Research, states that **"for every hour you exercise, you extend your life by two hours."** Many people are simply unaware of the negative consequences of an inactive lifestyle.

The value of a sound exercise program goes beyond the fact that it may allow you to live longer. As the following list of 100 reasons to exercise so vividly illustrates, exercise can also affect the quality of your life in many ways:

100 Reasons* To Make A Commitment to Total Fitness – TODAY!

1. Reduces your risk of getting heart disease.
2. Increases your level of muscle strength.
3. Improves the functioning of your immune system.
4. Enhances sexual desire, performance, and satisfaction.
5. Helps you to more effectively manage stress.
6. Helps you to lose weight - especially fat weight.
7. Improves the likelihood of survival from a myocardial infarction (heart attack).
8. Can help relieve the pain of tension headaches - perhaps the most common type of headache.
9. Improves your body's ability to use fat for energy during physical activity.
10. Increases the density and breaking strength of bones.
11. Helps to preserve lean body tissue.
12. Reduces the risk of developing hypertension (high blood pressure).
13. Increases the density and breaking strength of ligaments and tendons.
14. Improves coronary (heart) circulation.
15. Increases circulating levels of HDL (good) cholesterol.
16. Assists in efforts to stop smoking.
17. Reduces your risk of developing type II (non-insulin-dependent) diabetes.
18. Can help improve short-term memory in older individuals.
19. Helps to maintain weight loss - unlike dieting, alone.
20. Helps relieve many of the common discomforts of pregnancy (backache, heartburn, constipation, etc.).
21. Reduces your anxiety level.
22. Helps control blood pressure in people with hypertension.
23. Reduces the viscosity of your blood.
24. Reduces vulnerability to various cardiac dysrhythmias (abnormal heart rhythms).
25. Increases your maximal oxygen uptake (VO2 max—perhaps the best measure of your physical working capacity).
26. Helps to overcome jet lag.
27. Slows the rate of joint degeneration in people with osteoarthritis.
28. Lowers your resting heart rate.
29. Helps to boost creativity.
30. Reduces circulating levels of triglycerides.
31. Helps the body resist upper respiratory tract infections.
32. Increases your anaerobic threshold, allowing you to work or exercise longer at a higher level, before a significant amount of lactic acid builds up.

(* Written by Cedric X. Bryant and James A. Peterson; used with permission)

Table 2-1

33. Reduces medical and healthcare expenses.

34. Improves ability to recover from physical exertion.

35. Helps speed recovery from chemotherapy treatments.

36. Increases ability to supply blood to the skin for cooling.

37. Increases the thickness of the cartilage in your joints.

38. Gives you more energy to meet the demands of daily life, and provides you with a reserve to meet the demands of unexpected emergencies.

39. Increases your level of muscle endurance.

40. Helps you sleep easier and better.

41. Improves posture.

42. Improves athletic performance.

43. Helps you to maintain your resting metabolic rate.

44. Reduces the risk of developing colon cancer.

45. Increases your tissues' responsiveness to the actions of insulin (i.e., improves tissue sensitivity for insulin) helping to better control blood sugar, particularly if you are a Type II diabetic.

46. Helps to relieve constipation.

47. Expands blood plasma volume.

48. Reduces the risk of developing prostate cancer.

49. Helps to combat substance abuse.

50. Helps to alleviate depression.

51. Increases your ability to adapt to cold environments.

52. Helps you maintain proper muscle balance.

53. Reduces the rate and severity of medical complications associated with hypertension.

54. Helps to alleviate certain menstrual symptoms.

55. Lowers your heart rate response to submaximal physical exertion.

56. Helps to alleviate low-back pain.

57. Helps to reduce the amount of insulin required to control blood sugar levels in type I (insulin-dependent) diabetics.

58. Improves mental alertness.

59. Improves respiratory muscle strength and muscle endurance - particularly important for asthmatics.

60. Reduces your risk of having a stroke.

61. Helps you to burn excess calories.

62. Increases your cardiac reserve.

63. Improves your physical appearance.

64. Offsets some of the negative side effects of certain antihypertensive drugs.

65. Increases your stroke volume (the amount of blood the heart pumps with each beat).

66. Improves your self-esteem.

Table 2-1. (cont'd)

67. Reduces your susceptibility for coronary thrombosis (a clot in an artery that supplies the heart with blood).

68. Helps you to relax.

69. Reduces the risk of developing breast cancer.

70. Improves mental cognition (a short-term effect only).

71. Maintains or improves joint flexibility.

72. Improves your glucose tolerance.

73. Reduces workdays missed due to illness.

74. Protects against "creeping obesity" (the slow, but steady weight gain that occurs as you age).

75. Enhances your muscles' abilities to extract oxygen from your blood.

76. Increases your productivity at work.

77. Reduces your likelihood of developing low-back problems.

78. Improves your balance and coordination.

79. Allows you to consume greater quantities of food and still maintain caloric balance.

80. Provides protection against injury.

81. Decreases (by 20 to 30 percent) the need for antihypertensive medication, if you are hypertensive.

82. Improves your decision-making abilities.

83. Helps reduce and prevent the immediate symptoms of menopause (hot flashes, sleep disturbances, irritability) and decrease the long-term risks of cardiovascular disease, osteoporosis, and obesity.

84. Helps to relieve and prevent "migraine headache attacks."

85. Reduces the risk of endometriosis (a common cause of infertility).

86. Helps to retard bone loss as you age, thereby reducing your risk of developing osteoporosis.

87. Helps decrease your appetite (a short-term effect only).

88. Improves pain tolerance and mood if you suffer from osteoarthritis.

89. Helps prevent and relieve the stresses that cause carpal tunnel syndrome.

90. Makes your heart a more efficient pump.

91. Helps to decrease left ventricular hypertrophy (a thickening of the walls of the left ventricle) in people with hypertension.

92. Improves your mood

93. Helps to increase your overall health awareness.

94. Reduces the risk of gastrointestinal bleeding.

95. Lifelong regular exercise may help protect you against the development of Alzheimer's disease.

96. Reduces the level of abdominal obesity - a significant health-risk factor.

97. Increases the diffusion capacity of the lungs, enhancing the exchange of oxygen from your lungs to your blood.

98. Improves heat tolerance.

99. Improves your overall quality of life.

100. Helps you to maintain an independent lifestyle.

Table 2-1. (cont'd)

Translating Awareness Into Action

Obviously, it is not enough merely to be aware of the importance of a physically active lifestyle. In order to receive the vast array of benefits afforded by exercising, you have to engage in a sound exercise program on a regular basis. In this regard, the essential step, on your part, is to make a firm commitment to developing "total fitness."

Broadly defined, total fitness involves your ability to engage in activities of daily living without becoming too tired or being injured. If you are totally fit, you have the ability to do the things you need to do and like to do at work, home, and at play without a heightened risk of injury. Collectively, fitness is a by-product of four basic health-related components of fitness—cardiorespiratory fitness, muscular fitness, flexibility, and body composition. Health-related components of fitness are those factors that have an impact on your long-term health. In contrast, skill-related components of fitness (i.e., motor skills such as power, agility, coordination, kinesthetic awareness, balance, quickness, and foot speed) are important for performing athletic-type activities, but have little to do with your long-term health (Figure 2-1). Total health-related fitness is attained when all four health components are developed and maintained at an appropriate level. In this regard, the key point to remember is that you can be exceptionally fit in three of these components and not be totally fit. Total health-related fitness involves all four fitness elements.

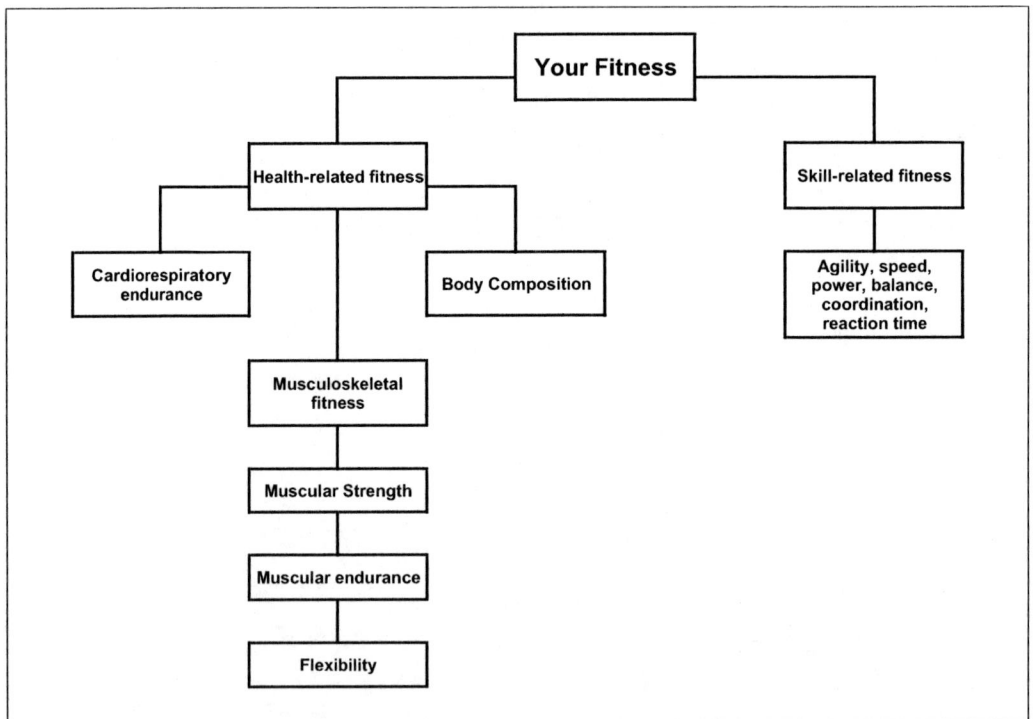

Figure 2-1. "Total Fitness" consists of both health related and skill related fitness

Cardiorespiratory fitness (sometimes referred to as aerobic fitness) is commonly defined as the coordinated ability of your pulmonary system (lungs), cardiovascular system (heart and blood vessels), and metabolic pathways within your muscular system to take in, deliver, and utilize oxygen. All factors considered, the more oxygen you can take in, deliver, and utilize, the more aerobically fit you are.

Muscular fitness can best be defined as the ability of your muscles to do what you want them to do when you need them to do it. Traditionally, many people view muscular fitness as encompassing two distinct applications of muscular work— muscular strength and muscular endurance. As such, muscular strength is defined as the ability of a muscle or muscle group to exert maximal force. Muscular endurance, on the other hand, can be defined as the ability of a muscle or a muscle group to exert submaximal force for an extended period of time.

Flexibility is generally defined as the ability of a skeletal joint to move through its full range of motion. Range of motion is highly specific to a given joint and is primarily dependent on the musculature that controls the movement of that joint. For example, being able to scratch the middle of your back is affected by the relative tightness of your shoulder muscles.

The fourth component of total health-related fitness is body composition—a relative indicator of the amount of fat stored in your body. In more specific terms, body composition is defined as the ratio of fat (adipose tissue) to fat-free mass (muscle, bone, water, and protein) in your body. Contrary to what most people believe, **it is not how much you weigh that is important to your health, its how much fat you have**. Considerable evidence shows that it is essential for your good health that you have an appropriate fat to fat free mass ratio, since an excessive level of fat has been found to be a significant risk factor for a number of diseases, including coronary heart disease, hypertension, and diabetes.

While each component is a distinct entity unto itself, performing activities of daily living involves the simultaneous interaction of all four health components. As such, your life can be viewed as a synergistic environment in which you need each of these components at various times, in varying degrees.

Obviously, how these components interact can vary from task-to-task, individual-to-individual, and situation-to-situation. For example, at a minimum, carrying groceries up several flights of stairs can require both cardiorespiratory fitness and muscular fitness. In turn, putting those groceries away in an overhead cabinet can involve flexibility, as well as muscular fitness.

Making Exercise Work For You

From a physical and mental health standpoint, a physically active life can easily be distinguished from a sedentary one. Fortunately, a healthier tomorrow is well within your reach. The key is making a commitment to be fit. Such an undertaking can be more easily achieved and maintained if you adopt a commonsense approach, including start exercising today (i.e., stop procrastinating); focus on making relatively small changes over time in your physical activity patterns; exercise with a partner who can help encourage and support your efforts and make your exercise efforts enjoyable. Exercise does not—should not—have to involve drudgery; don't punish yourself if you have temporary setbacks in your exercise efforts. In other words, do everything possible to enhance your level of fitness. In the process, you'll find that exercising on a regular basis is one of the best things you will ever do for yourself.

CHAPTER THREE

UNDERSTANDING YOUR

HEALTH RISK FACTORS

The key is to know as much as possible about your health risk factors in order to better understand the consequences of your behavioral choices.

Unsafe. Chancy. Dangerous. Perilous. All words with a potentially negative or threatening connotation—particularly if they're used to describe an action or a specific lifestyle choice on your part that might affect your health or how long you live. As a point of fact, a number of risk factors have been identified that can have an impact on your health and on your level of longevity.

The key is to know as much a possible about your health risk factors (Figure 3-1) in order to better understand the consequences of your behavioral choices. While your health risk factors may indicate that you are at risk for certain diseases and medical conditions, you have the ability to do something about minimizing your level of risk. Fortunately, except for whatever risk you have that is due to genetic factors (heredity, gender, and age), you have the opportunity to control most of the factors placing your health at risk. In other words, to a point, you have the capacity to manage your health.

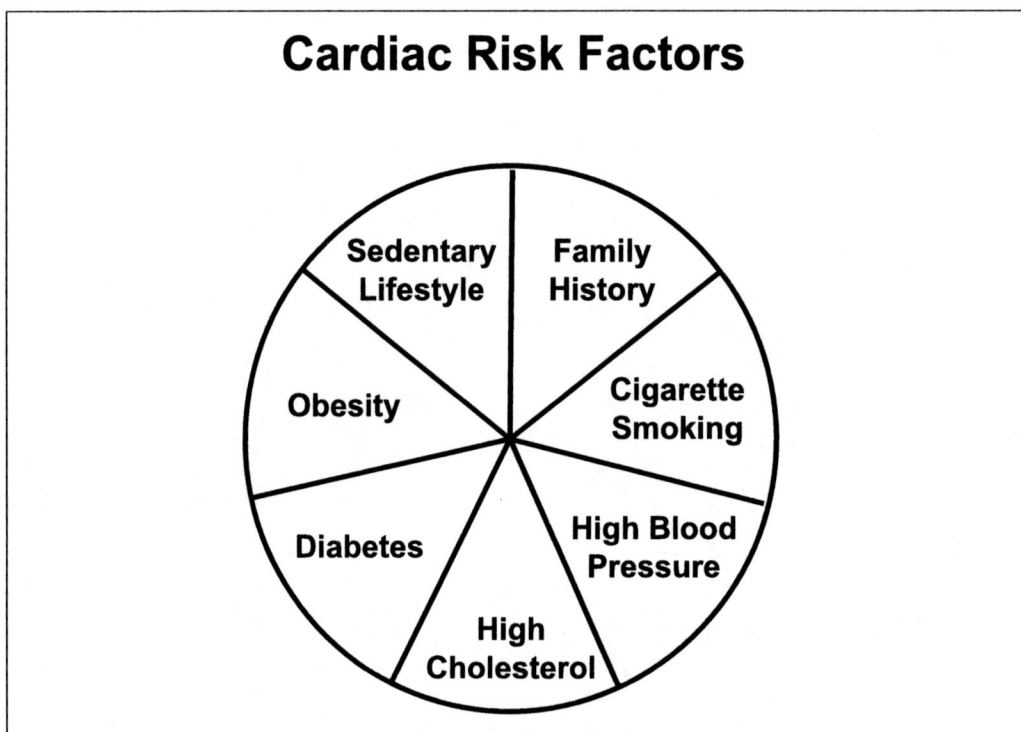

Cardiac Risk Factors

Sedentary Lifestyle · Family History · Obesity · Cigarette Smoking · Diabetes · High Blood Pressure · High Cholesterol

Figure 3-1. Except for family history, sex, and age, you have the opportunity to control most of the factors placing your health at risk

Collectively, your health risk factors also provide you with a sense (i.e., profile) of how serious your health risks are. In turn, your health risk profile can be used to determine whether you can safely engage in an exercise program without seeing a physician or taking a graded exercise test beforehand.

Understanding the Inherent Risk Factors to Your Health

Everyday living carries with it inherent risks to your health. Certainly living in an environment with air pollution, exposing yourself to the dangers of freeway commuting, and enduring the stressors of a highly competitive workplace can all contribute to the risk of premature negative health conditions. When the most debilitating diseases (those that are directly responsible for the majority of premature disabilities and death) are examined closely, however, eight health risk factors are associated with them. Three of these factors are out of your control; the other five can be modified.

Uncontrollable Risk Factors

The three health risk factors beyond your control are age, sex, and family history. Age and sex interact, while family history stands alone. Understanding the specifics of these three factors can enable you to be better able to deal with their ramifications for your health.

Age/sex: Men over 45 years of age and women older than 55 (or post-menopausal women without estrogen replacement therapy) are at greater risk for debilitating disease than the general population.

Family history: Individuals who have fathers or close male relatives who have had heart attacks or sudden death before age 55, or who have mothers or other close female relatives who've experienced the same condition(s) prior to 65 years of age, are at greater risk for serious disease than others.

Although there is nothing you can do about these three uncontrollable risk factors, recognizing them can help you better understand the importance of exerting control over the five factors that you CAN modify:

Controllable Risk Factors

Although a number of factors exist that are associated with disease and disability (and there are certainly others that will be discovered over the coming years), the most clearly understood of the controllable health risk factors are high blood pressure, high blood cholesterol, diabetes, cigarette smoking, and sedentary lifestyle.

High blood pressure: Also called hypertension, high blood pressure is a significant health risk factor. It is defined as a blood pressure greater than 140 over 90. The larger number is referred to as systolic blood pressure. Systolic blood pressure measures the pressure in the blood vessels at the moment of heart contraction (heart beat). The smaller number is referred to as diastolic pressure. Diastolic blood pressure measures the pressure in the blood vessels between heart contractions. Keep in mind that the higher your level of blood pressure, the greater amount of work your heart has to do.

While such a situation may not be a significant problem for you currently, it can unduly tax (overwork) your heart in the long run.

Sometimes referred to as the "silent killer", hypertension typically doesn't have outward symptoms. Therefore, it's important that blood pressure be monitored regularly during treatment. In that regard, exercise can have a positive impact on your blood pressure level (i.e., all other factors considered, people who exercise have a lower blood pressure than their sedentary counterparts). In addition to exercise, other common treatments for blood pressure higher than 140 systolic or 90 diastolic are the avoidance of stress-causing environments and other types of stress management strategies, reduction of salt in your diet, reduction of body fat, and prescription medication. In some cases, a combination of these strategies is utilized.

High blood cholesterol: High serum cholesterol is an important risk factor when it is greater than 200. As your total cholesterol rises above this value, your risk for premature disease raises with it. Since it is known that a portion of total cholesterol actually protects AGAINST coronary artery disease, to a degree, using total cholesterol levels as a measure of health risk is acceptable if a lipid (type of fat) breakdown is not available. In that regard, if your total cholesterol is between 200 and 240, your health risk would be considered borderline. Above 240, your health risk would be judged as high.

If a lipid analysis is available, a better way to analyze your health risk is by determining the amount of high density lipoprotein (HDL cholesterol)—typically referred to as "good cholesterol"—that makes up the total amount of cholesterol in your blood. Generally speaking, if your HDL level is less than 40 mg/dl, your blood does not have enough good cholesterol in it, and you have a significant health risk for coronary heart disease. On the other hand, if your HDL levels are higher than 60 mg/dl, or if your ratio of total serum cholesterol to HDL is less than four to five, your risk of coronary heart disease actually decreases.

Diabetes: One of the risk categories that indicates the need for medical clearance prior to engaging in an exercise program is the category "with disease". Individuals with insulin dependent diabetes mellitus (type I diabetes—commonly referred to as juvenile diabetes) who are less than 30 years of age, or who have had the disease for more than 15 years, and persons with non-insulin dependent diabetes mellitus (type II diabetes—commonly referred to as adult-onset diabetes) who are over 35 years of age are classified as patients with disease. Both types of the disease result in elevated blood sugar levels. In Type I diabetes, this elevation is caused by a dysfunctional pancreas. In Type II diabetes, the elevated blood sugar level is caused by a decreased sensitivity to insulin in the peripheral tissues. In general, type II diabetes is directly related to an individual's inactive lifestyle and amount of relative obesity. Eighty to ninety percent of Type 2 diabetics (adult onset) are overweight. Either form of the disease is a significant health risk factor.

Cigarette smoking: Smoking cigarettes is a pervasive risk factor because it increases your health risk in proportion to the quantity of cigarettes you smoke. Since the nicotine in cigarettes is addictive, and because your body adapts to nicotine levels rather quickly, greater and greater amounts of nicotine are required to satisfy your addiction. Unless you stop smoking, your addiction can lead to a negative spiral of more smoking, more need for nicotine, and greater health loss. Some of the consequences of smoking are decreased delivery of oxygen to your brain and peripheral organs, increased stress on your coronary vessels and the cardiac tissue itself, increased rate of atherosclerosis, and an increased inflammation of your pulmonary tissue, resulting in a variety of diseases involving your lungs. Smokers increase their risk of heart disease 1.7 – 2.4x's over a non-smoker.

Sedentary lifestyle: Long-range, medically-based studies of all-cause mortality point out the importance of NOT being sedentary. When the exercise habits of both men and women are examined over years of research, one of the most conclusive recommendations relative to the relationship between activity of lifestyle and amount of premature death or disability is "STAY OUT OF THE SEDENTARY LIFESTYLE CATEGORY!!" Probably the most interesting finding of this research is that the most important predictor of living longer is not to be classified in the lowest fitness category. Although additional levels of fitness may increase how long you live somewhat, they will not increase it substantially. In other words, systematic exercise at relatively low levels will increase how long you live almost as much as more vigorous exercise. In that regard, **an obese individual who exercises on a regular basis may be at a lower level of health risk than an inactive low fat person who never exercises.**

The Role of Exercise in Reducing Your Health Risk

Understanding your health risks is just the beginning. Once you understand the risks you're facing, you need to figure out a way to get them under control. One of the best ways to manage your health risk factors is through regular physical activity. Hundreds of research studies over the years support the following conclusions relative to blood pressure, serum cholesterol, diabetes, cigarette smoking, and sedentary lifestyle:

Blood pressure reduction: Both systolic and diastolic blood pressure are decreased through regular physical activity. Since any reduction in blood pressure is associated with lower risk, beginning or maintaining a regular physical fitness program is a positive strategy for managing your blood pressure.

Cholesterol management: As with blood pressure, decreases in total cholesterol result in decreases in disease risk. Specifically, for every one-percent decrease in total serum cholesterol, mortality from coronary artery disease declines about two percent. The chief role of exercise in total serum cholesterol management is based on the associated weight loss due to exercise.

More important than total cholesterol, however, is the role of exercise in raising your HDL levels of cholesterol (good cholesterol). HDL has been shown to increase with exercise training and is typically at high levels in endurance-trained individuals. In this regard, exercise raises the amount of your HDL cholesterol without affecting total cholesterol. In other words, what exercise does is lower your cholesterol:HDL ratio. The lower your cholesterol:HDL ratio, the lower your risk of premature disease.

Diabetes and weight control: Exercise has been shown to positively affect the health risk of individuals with diabetes, particularly those with Type II, or adult-onset, diabetes. Probably the greatest role of exercise in managing diabetes is in helping individuals with diabetes to control their body weight. There is a positive correlation between individuals who engage in regular physical activity, and the degree to which they maintain a healthy amount of body weight.

Exercise and smoking: Because smoking and exercise are such incompatible behaviors, exercise can be a real aid in your efforts to quit a nicotine habit. One way that exercise can help individuals attempt to quit smoking is by eliminating one of the excuses that smokers use not to quit—namely, that people who stop smoking inevitably gain weight. In reality, a sound exercise regimen performed in conjunction with a smoking cessation program can help keep you from gaining weight. Any additional calories that you might consume as part of the fact that you go through the nicotine withdrawal process are "neutralized" by the increased energy expenditure that results from exercising. In addition to the fact that exercise helps burn additional calories, anecdotal evidence exists that exercise helps nicotine quitters "blow off" nervous energy associated with nicotine withdrawal.

Sedentary lifestyle, disease, and exercise: A relationship between a sedentary lifestyle, heart disease, and all-cause mortality has also been found. More importantly, considerable evidence exists that indicates that some exercise is better than no exercise relative to the prevention of disease. Exercise, by definition, directly counters the health risks of an inactive lifestyle; and, at the same time, exercise influences almost all of the other risk factors for chronic disease. When employed in conjunction with a sound nutrition and behavior modification program, exercise can be a powerful intervention tool against premature chronic disease.

The point to keep in mind is that regular physical activity has numerous benefits with regard to reducing your health risk, including:

- improves your cardiorespiratory efficiency by increasing the amount of oxygen that your body can utilize

- lowers your heart rate and blood pressure

- increases your work threshold for the accumulation of waste products in your muscles (thus allowing greater amounts of work before fatigue sets in)

- increases your work threshold for the onset of disease symptoms

- reduces systolic and diastolic blood pressure

- increases your level of HDL cholesterol

- reduces your body fat

- reduces your insulin needs (improves your glucose or blood sugar tolerance)

- reduces the likelihood that you will die from coronary artery disease

- helps you live longer.

- decreases your feelings of anxiety and depression

- improves your feelings of well-being

- enhances your ability to perform work, recreational, and sports activities

Exercise Intensity

Your risk factor profile is important in deciding if you need medical screening prior to engaging in certain types of exercise intensity. As mentioned previously, the intensity of your exercise activities is another factor that needs to be considered to determine if you need additional medical screening prior to beginning your exercise program. The American College of Sports Medicine (ACSM) defines two categories of exercise intensity; moderate or vigorous activity.

Moderate Intensity

Moderate intensity activities are well within your current capacity and can be sustained comfortably for a prolonged period (an hour straight, for example). Activities that fall within this category of intensity are steady walking, easy cycling, light stair climbing, low- or no-impact aerobic classes, senior strength and stretch classes, easy-lap swimming, etc. The key variables in this category are comfort and duration. In other words, the exercise activities you choose can be performed continuously and comfortably for an extended period of time.

Vigorous Activity

Vigorous intensity can be defined as activities that can be continuously maintained for 30-40 minutes at or near a pace where you can hold a conversation with a friend or fitness professional. High intensity types of activities, on the other hand, cause significant increases in your heart rate and respiration rate; and they usually cannot be sustained for more than 15-20 minutes by untrained individuals. Examples of exercises representative of vigorous and high-intensity are jogging, aerobic dance, stair climbing, step aerobics, active sports and games, and most types of traditional weight lifting.

Determining Your Risk Profile

Given the discussion of health-risk categories and the different intensity levels of your intended exercise program, the next step is to determine your personal risk profile. Keeping in mind both uncontrollable and controllable risk factors and the intensity of the exercise program you are about to begin, addressing the issues raised in the following sections (age, physical activity readiness questionnaire, coronary risk factor profile) will allow you to place yourself in one of the ACSM risk categories. Once you "fall into" one of the categories, you should follow the aforementioned recommendations relative to your need for medical screening before you begin your exercise program.

Age Criterion

ACSM has established the following guideline with regard to your age and the level of intensity of your proposed exercise program:

> ***It is recommended that all males over 45 and females over 55 undergo medical evaluation and/or diagnostic exercise testing prior to beginning or participating in moderate or vigorous intensity exercise activities.***

If the above age criterion does not apply to you, you should determine the intensity level you intend to exercise. If your planned intensity level is low to moderate, you should answer the questions in chapter four from the Physical Activity Readiness Questionnaire (PAR-Q). If you plan to participate in activities at high or vigorous" levels of intensity, you should consult your medical professional prior to initiating a program.

The Chance of a Lifetime

It is apparent that exercise is good for you. It is even more clear, however, that a sound exercise program initiated after a medical consultation is simply the safest and most sensible course of action. Only after you've been medically cleared to exercise are you ready to begin a graduated program of cardiorespiratory, strength, and flexibility activities, as described in subsequent chapters in this book. At You Turn, we strongly believe ignoring your health risk factors is a gamble that should not be undertaken.

CHAPTER FOUR

DETERMINING

HOW FIT YOU ARE

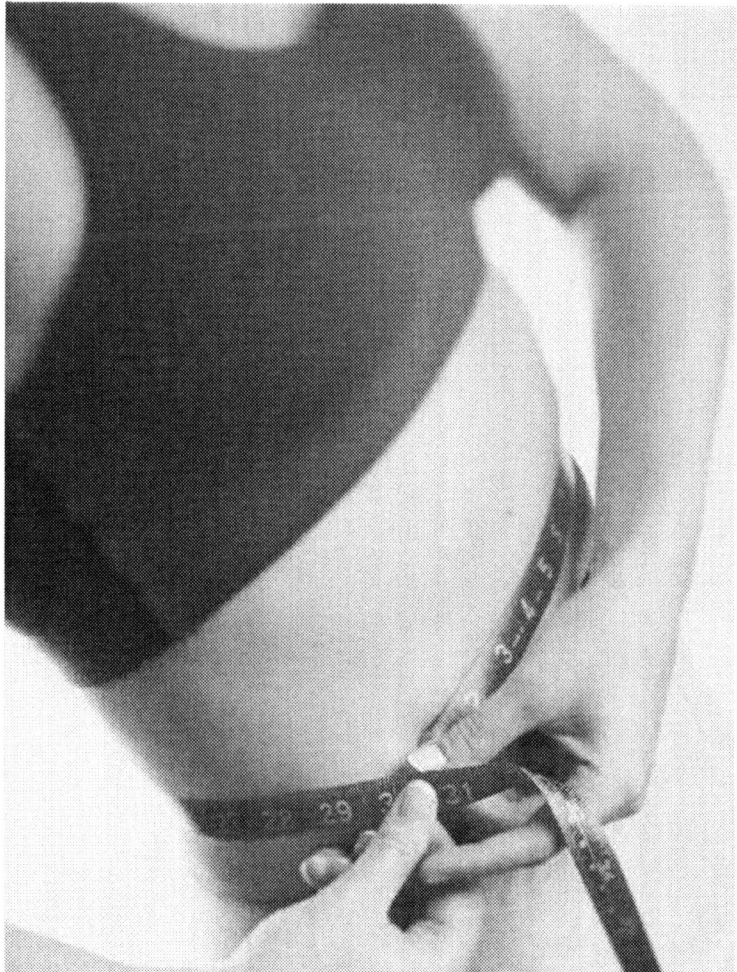

If you want to maximize the capacity of your body to withstand the demands imposed upon it by your lifestyle (work, home, play), you should periodically check out your level of physical fitness.

The need to be aware of your "situation" starts early in most people's lives. Look both ways before you cross the street. Check with your parents before you make plans. Check out your appearance before you leave for school in the morning.

As you get older, the need to continuously check things out becomes more of a concern. Check out the traffic before you change lanes. Check out the price of comparable items before you make a purchase. Check out your alternatives before you accept a job. Undergo a health examination annually.

In a similar vein, it could be reasonably argued that if you want to maximize the capacity of your body to withstand the demands imposed upon it by your lifestyle (work, home play), you should periodically check out your level of physical fitness. Although you may think you know how fit you are, a more structured evaluation can offer you a quantified basis for deciding whether you need to take specific steps to remedy a functional deficiency. Later, information you obtain from such an assessment can also help provide a basis for evaluating how well your conditioning efforts are working. Keep in mind that it's never too late to test yourself. Furthermore, you don't need to be fit or of a particular age to be tested. If the tests for checking out your level of fitness provide you with meaningful feedback, you have everything to gain and nothing to lose.

Do you have difficulty moving a heavy object from one point to another? Do you have the energy to do the things you like to do? Do you have trouble lifting something over your head? Do you often suffer from nagging aches and pains? In other words, is your body capable of handling the demands of your lifestyle? To what degree? How do you know? Are you sure? Is there anything you can do to be sure? Surprisingly enough, the easiest approach to answering these questions is relatively straightforward.

One of the most productive steps you can take in this regard is to determine how fit you are and to then do whatever is necessary to improve your level of fitness. Since the methods that can be used to assess your level of fitness vary considerably in their ease of administration, cost, and degree of accuracy, you need to carefully consider your testing options.

What You Should Test

Your initial task should be to determine what factors or measures to test. The most popular approach is to separately assess the four basic health-related components of total fitness (cardiorespiratory fitness, muscular fitness, flexibility, and body composition).

Why You Should Assess Your Fitness

The results of your assessment efforts can give you a "sense" of your fitness profile. Your test results can also be helpful to you in other ways. At a minimum, your test scores can help you develop a personalized exercise program. Periodic testing can also enable you to monitor your progress in your conditioning regimen and to determine to what degree you are achieving your fitness goals. Accordingly, your assessment results can let you know whether adjustments in your training program need to be made. Finally, your fitness evaluation can provide you with a "snapshot" of any fitness-associated issues that may be facing you in later life.

The Key to Successful Testing

In order to make your testing efforts as productive as possible, you need to use proven, meaningful methods to assess each of the four basic components of total fitness. You then need to take whatever steps are necessary to ensure that each test is conducted properly. Keep in mind that if you compromise the proper way to perform a specific test, you compromise the usefulness of any information that you might get from that test.

A number of assessment tests and procedures are available to test each component of fitness. At You Turn, individuals undergo a variety of tests, including a sub-maximal cycle ergometer or treadmill test to evaluate cardiorespiratory fitness, resting and exercise heart rate and blood pressure, a sit-and-reach test to assess trunk flexibility, tests for both muscular strength (bench press and leg press) and muscular endurance (sit-ups or push-ups) and a body composition evaluation (percentage of body fat and lean muscle mass) by either bioelectrical impedance, skinfold testing or measuring the circumference of various body areas.

How Aerobically Fit Are You?

Cardiorespiratory fitness (commonly referred to as "aerobic fitness") is a reflection of your body's ability to take in, deliver, and utilize oxygen during endurance activities such as walking, jogging, swimming and cycling. All factors considered, the better your body's pulmonary system (lungs), cardiovascular system (heart and blood vessels), and metabolic pathways within your muscular system accomplish these tasks, the more aerobically fit you are.

The most widely accepted measure of aerobic fitness is based upon how much physical activity you can do before you become fatigued. This measure is commonly referred to as your level of maximal oxygen uptake — $\dot{V}O_2max$. There are numerous ways to determine the $\dot{V}O_2max$ including estimating maximal oxygen uptake, conducting a sub maximal test and predicting maximum from the sub maximal data and measuring the individuals maximal performance directly. When conducted in a You Turn location, $\dot{V}O_2max$ testing usually involves the direct measurement of the gases you exhale while exercising during a sub maximal effort. Analyzing your exhaled oxygen and carbon dioxide levels has been shown to provide a very accurate measurement of your $\dot{V}O_2max$.

There are also simple, non-laboratory methods for determining your level of $\dot{V}O_2$max. This simplified approach involves predicting your $\dot{V}O_2$max on the basis of either how well you perform a specific task. For instance, how fast can you walk or run a specific distance? How much does your heart rate change during submaximal exercise? Fitness testing (and retesting) can be useful to illustrate gains and improvements that have been made in your "total fitness".

Safety first. Prior to taking a physically challenging exercise test, you should take certain precautions whether you are scheduled to take the test in a health related facility or not. At a facility, these precautions should involve completing a health/medical questionnaire, having your resting blood pressure and resting heart rate measured, and signing an informed consent form.

One of the most widely used health/medical questionnaires today is the Physical Activity Readiness Questionnaire (PAR-Q), a relatively simple yet quite valid form that is used to screen individuals prior to their undergoing exercise testing or initiating an exercise program (a PAR-Q is shown in Table 4-1). The PAR-Q has been widely used over the years to determine whether it is safe for you to engage in a physically demanding activity.

A "yes" answer to any of the seven questions on the PAR-Q should disqualify you from taking part in an exercise test or exercise program until you have obtained appropriate medical clearance. If you did not answer yes to any of the questions on the PAR-Q, you are considered as an apparently healthy person. As such, it's acceptable for you to be tested either in a health club by a trained professional or on your own.

Assessing aerobic fitness in a health club setting. Since laboratory testing of aerobic fitness is not affordable for the majority of individuals, several tests to predict VO2 max have been developed for a health club setting. Among the more commonly employed tests are performance-based measures and tests that use your heart rate response to a submaximal walking or running exercise bout as the primary indicator.

How Muscularly Fit Are You?

Daily living activities (at home, work, and play) require you to use your muscles. The muscles must be capable of doing what you want them to do when you need them to do it and for the length of time you want them to without sustaining an injury. This capability is typically referred to as muscular fitness.

The exercise science communities consider muscular fitness as a combination of two distinct applications: muscular strength and muscular endurance. Muscular strength is the ability of a muscle or a muscle group to exert a short-term maximum force. Muscular endurance, on the other hand, is the ability of a muscle or a muscle

Physical Activity Readiness
Questionnaire-PAR-Q
(revised 1994)

PAR-Q & YOU

(A Questionnaire for People Aged 15 to 69)

Regular physical activity is fun and healthy, and increasingly more people are starting to become more active every day. Being more active is very safe for most people. However, some people should check with their doctor before they start becoming much more physically active.

If you are planning to become much more physically active than you are now, start by answering the seven questions in the box below. If you are between the ages of 15 and 69, the PAR-Q will tell you if you should check with your doctor before you start. If you are over 69 years of age, and you are not used to being very active, check with your doctor.

Common sense is your best guide when you answer these questions. Please read the questions carefully and answer each one honestly: check YES or NO.

YES	NO	
☐	☐	1. Has your doctor ever said that you have a heart condition *and* that you should only do physical activity recommended by a doctor?
☐	☐	2. Do you feel pain in your chest when you do physical activity?
☐	☐	3. In the past month, have you had chest pain when you were not doing physical activity?
☐	☐	4. Do you lose your balance because of dizziness or do you ever lose consciousness?
☐	☐	5. Do you have a bone or joint problem that could be made worse by a change in your physical activity?
☐	☐	6. Is your doctor currently prescribing drugs (for example, water pills) for your blood pressure or heart condition?
☐	☐	7. Do you know of any *other reason* why you should not do physical activity?

If

you

answered

YES to one or more questions

Talk with your doctor by phone or in person BEFORE you start becoming much more physically active or BEFORE you have a fitness appraisal. Tell your doctor about the PAR-Q and which questions you answered YES.

- You may be able to do any activity you want—as long as you start slowly and build up gradually. Or, you may need to restrict your activities to those which are safe for you. Talk with your doctor about the kinds of activities you wish to participate in and follow his/her advice.
- Find out which community programs are safe and helpful for you.

NO to all questions

If you answered NO honestly to *all* PAR-Q questions, you can be reasonably sure that you can:

- start becoming much more physically active—begin slowly and build up gradually. This is the safest and easiest way to go.
- take part in the fitness appraisal—this is an excellent way to determine your basic fitness so that you can plan the best way for you to live actively.

DELAY BECOMING MUCH MORE ACTIVE:
- If you are not feeling well because of a temporary illness such as a cold or a fever—wait until you feel better; or
- If you are or may be pregnant—talk to your doctor before you start becoming more active.

Please note: If your health changes so that you then answer YES to any of the above questions, tell your fitness or health professional. Ask whether you should change your physical activity plan.

Informed Use of the PAR-Q: The Canadian Society for Exercise Physiology, Health Canada, and their agents assume no liability for persons who undertake physical activity, and if in doubt after completing this questionnaire, consult your doctor prior to physical activity.

You are encouraged to copy the PAR-Q but only if you use the entire form.

Note: If the PAR-Q is being given to a person before he or she participates in a physical activity program or a fitness appraisal, this section may be used for legal or administrative purposes.

I have read, understood and completed this questionnaire. Any questions I had were answered to my full satisfaction.

NAME _____

SIGNATURE _____ DATE _____

SIGNATURE OF PARENT _____ WITNESS _____
or GUARDIAN (for participants under the age of majority)

© Canadian Society for Exercise Physiology
Société canadienne de physiologie de l'exercice   Supported by: Health   Santé
         Canada   Canada

Reprinted from the 1994 revised version of the Physical Activity Readiness Questionnaire (PAR-Q and YOU). The PAR-Q and YOU is a copyrighted, pre-exercise screen owned by the Canadian Society for Exercise Physiology.

Table 4-1. PAR-Q and You

group to exert submaximal force for an extended period of time. Accordingly, the first step in assessing muscular fitness involves identifying which application of muscular fitness you wish to measure—strength or endurance.

Generally, muscular fitness is assessed using tests that either employ specific devices for measuring muscular strength and muscular endurance or involve performing calisthenic-type exercises. Calisthenic-type tests usually require little or no equipment, can be performed almost anywhere, and involves bodily movements which are somewhat more functional in nature.

Given the fact that individuals have their own unique genetic potential for achieving and demonstrating muscular fitness, comparing the muscular fitness assessment results of one person to another is of questionable value. A more logical approach would be to compare the results of your muscular fitness testing to your previous performances. Even accounting for the occasional glitch in testing results that might be attributed to emotional or physical factors, comparing the results of your assessment efforts with your previous test scores should provide you with a reasonable basis for measuring the progress of your training efforts over the long haul.

How Flexible Are You?

Flexibility is the capacity of a skeletal joint to move through its full range of motion. This health-related fitness component is important to you for a number of reasons—not the least of which is that, all factors considered, a flexible muscle is less likely to be pulled or strained or to place undue pressure on a particular area of your body (e.g., your lower back, your shoulders, etc.). How flexible you are is related to the relative "tightness" of the various soft tissues of your skeletal joints (joint capsule, muscles, tendons, ligaments). The musculature supporting a specific joint is the primary factor affecting how well that joint can move through its full range of motion.

The analogy of a muscle being like a rubber band can help explain a muscle's affect on the flexibility level of one of your skeletal joints. If you pull a little on the rubber band and then let go, you create a certain amount of movement and energy. If you pull a lot, you have even greater movement and energy. On the other hand, if you pull too much or you can't pull it at all, you respectively break the rubber band (muscle) or fail to generate any movement or energy.

Because flexibility is specific to a given joint, no general flexibility test exists for your total body. As a consequence, you need to assess separately the flexibility of each of your skeletal joints.

Flexibility is sometimes assessed through a medical device specifically designed to measure the range of motion of a particular joint (called a goniometer). More typically, individuals tested in a club setting use a device called a sit and reach box, a linear

Flexibility is a major component of total fitness.

measurement of a joints range of motion. This test is completed with an individual seated on the floor with legs together, flat against the floor and both feet pointing straight up in the air. The individual will try to lean forward as far as possible and a measurement is taken as to how far away or past the toes an individual can achieve.

How Much Fat is Too Much Fat?

Having an appropriate level of body composition (i.e., the ratio of fat to fat-free mass in your body) is important to you for a number of reasons—some physical, some mental. An excessive level of fat has been shown to be a major cause of several diseases, including diabetes, cardiovascular disease and many cancers. Too much body fat can also have a negative impact on how you feel about yourself and how easily you are able to interact with others in a social setting.

Perhaps the most commonly employed and certainly the easier method for determining your relative level of body composition is to simply look at yourself in a full-length mirror without any clothes on. If you don't like what you see, you may have too much fat.

Quantitatively, you can measure your body composition with a variety of methods. The most practical method of assessing body composition is to use one of the several non-laboratory options (e.g., skinfold testing, circumference measurements, bioelectrical impedance, waist-to-hip ratio, etc.).

Skinfold testing. Skinfold testing involves measuring the amount of skin and fat just beneath the skin at any given location on your body. This test is conducted by pinching your skin at a pre-selected site (everything but muscle) and then measuring the thickness of the pinch. If you have someone else conduct the skinfold testing or take the circumstance measurements (as is the usual case), you should ensure that the person doing the testing has done such testing before and that you receive a test-retest, in order to validate the results of your testing. Furthermore, your test-retest should be conducted by the same individual.

The data from pre-selected skinfold site pinches (triceps, chest, abdomen, thigh) is then factored into specific equations that are designed to calculate your body composition. A number of different skinfold test equations exist. Keep in mind, when deciding whether to use a particular equation that most equations are gender- and age-specific and are designed to be employed only with a population similar to that from which they were derived. Each equation is based on data collected on specific body sites and requires precise techniques for measuring the skinfolds at each such site.

Circumference measurements. According to the circumference method for estimating percent body fat, large circumferences at certain sites on your body (e.g., waist, hips, etc.) indicate a higher level of percent body fat, while large circumferences at other sites (e.g., your neck) indicate a lower level of percent body fat. A number of equations employ circumference measurements (typically made with a cloth measuring tape that does not stretch when pulled). Each equation involves specific measurements and detailed techniques for taking those measurements.

Bioelectrical impedance is based upon the principle that the conductivity of an electrical impulse is greater through lean muscle mass than fatty tissue. When a miniscule electrical charge is sent through the body, a computer measures the resistance between electrodes and computes body density and therefore body composition.

Waist-to-hip ratio. Many researchers have concluded that your level of percent body fat is probably not as important as where the fat is located on your body. Collectively, where the fat is deposited on your body is often referred to as fat patterning. Your fat distribution patterns can predict your susceptibility to certain medical problems. Fat stored in your abdominal region, for example, as opposed to your legs, hips, and arms, indicates susceptibility to coronary disease.

Fat patterning can also label individuals according to the "shape" of their body. For example, if you tend to store excess fat on your chest and stomach areas, you are termed an "apple" (because an apple is wider at the top than at the bottom). If you have excess fat below your waist, you are a "pear" (a pear is wider at the bottom than at the top).

A relatively easy-to-perform field test of your fat distribution pattern is your waist-to-hip ratio (WHR). Simply stated, this ratio compares the narrowest portion of your waist (the circumference of your body measured at the level of your bellybutton) to the widest area of your hips (the circumference of your body measured at the largest protrusion of your buttocks). The larger the ratio, the higher the level of fat deposited on your waist. In turn, the larger the ratio, the higher your risk of certain medical problems. A cut-off ratio of 0.80 for men and 0.95 for women has been established as the maximal WHR limit, above which your risk for heart disease becomes substantially higher.

The Bottom Line

Once you've made a commitment to exercise on a regular basis, assessing your fitness level is and excellent first step on the road to good health. The results of your fitness testing not only can be used to tell you what shape you're actually in, but also provide insight into what shape you should be in (by comparing your results to national norms). The information gained from your fitness testing can also serve as the basis for determining what you should do (i.e., your exercise prescriptions) to transform your fitness level from where it is presently to where you want it to be in the future. In other words, is fitness testing worth the time and effort? The bottom-line answer—"certainly."

CHAPTER FIVE

ESTABLISHING

YOUR FITNESS GOALS

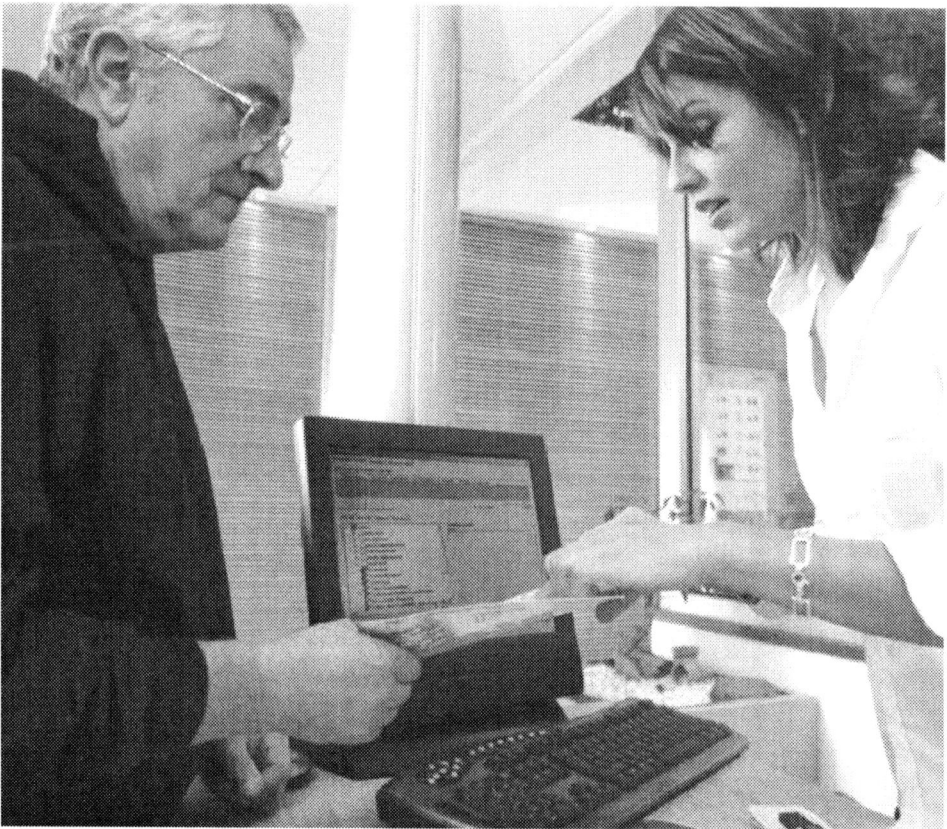

Identifying your fitness goals enables you to establish a basis for determining what activities should be a part of your exercise regimen, and also helps set up criteria for evaluating how well your program is working.

Once you've determined how fit you are, the logical next step is to determine what goals you would like to achieve from your exercise efforts. Identifying your fitness goals enables you to establish a basis for determining what activities should be part of your exercise regimen and also helps set up criteria for evaluating how well your program is working. Keep in mind that it didn't take two weeks for you to get into your current level of condition, and you shouldn't try to get "in shape" in two weeks.

Establishing your personal fitness goals can benefit you in other ways as well. For example, determining the objectives you plan to accomplish by exercising can help to provide you with the motivation to make meaningful changes in the physical activity level of your life and to stick with those changes. Knowing "where" you are in life in terms of fitness is usually not enough. You must also know where you should be before you can script a "road map" for getting there. Your exercise program goals can help serve as the directional bridge between "what is" and "what can ultimately be" with regard to your level of fitness and health.

What Is a Fitness Goal?

A fitness goal is simply a statement of results that you want to achieve from your exercise program. Establishing a fitness goal involves identifying some specific measurable accomplishment you hope to achieve within specific time and resource constraints. Such an objective should address four major elements: (1) an action or accomplishment verb; (2) a single, measurable, significant result; (3) a time period or date within which or by which the result is to be achieved; and (4) the outlay of resources (time, money, etc.) that you expect or are willing to commit to making the desired result a reality.

Using the aforementioned model as a guideline, you can construct a fitness goal that will meet your unique objectives and situation. For example:

- To lose ten pounds within 30 days by watching what you eat and working out on a treadmill three times per week, 20 minutes per session

- To lower your blood pressure to within a normal range within six months by stopping smoking, making a conscious effort to eat a healthier diet, and exercise regularly at least four times a week for a minimum of 30 minutes per session.

- To be able to do at least twenty properly-performed push-ups non-stop by your next birthday by engaging in a sound, total-body strength training workout.

You should note that none of the three sample personal fitness goals includes a justification for its existence or a precise description of how it should be accomplished.

As a rule, a fitness goal identifies only what, when, and how much exercise is involved. The "why" comes before (refer to Chapters 1, 2 and 3) and the prescription for "how" comes afterward (refer to Chapter 6).

How Do You Set Your Fitness Goals?

Deciding what you want to achieve from your exercise efforts is a personal matter. Obviously, you can and should consider feedback from individuals who are in a position to give you thoughtful advice (e.g., your physician, a personal trainer, close friends, etc.). On the other hand, who is better qualified than you to decide what your interests and needs are relative to your exercise program.

At You Turn, we like to take the S.M.A.R.T. approach to goal setting This practical acronym offers five basic criteria that each of your fitness goals should meet:

Specific

Measurable

Appropriate

Realistic

Timely

- Specific. Your fitness goal needs to identify exactly what objective you hope to achieve by exercising on a regular basis. Although you can have more than one goal, each particular goal should specify a single key result to be accomplished (e.g., lose weight, develop strength, lower resting heart rate, etc.). You should be able to look at the one key objective and tell the extent to which your goal has been achieved.

- Measurable. Whenever possible, through the use of numbers or percentages, you should quantify your fitness goals (e.g., lose 10 pounds, bench press your body weight, lower your resting heart rate at least 5bpm, etc.). Quantifying your goals makes it easier for you to determine the relative extent to which your exercise efforts are successful.

- Appropriate. Your fitness goals should be appropriate to your personal interests and needs. At the least, none of your fitness goals should expose you to an undue likelihood of doing anything that might otherwise subject you to any injury or health problem (e.g., losing too much weight, losing a significant amount of weight too fast, placing too much stress on your joints, etc.). The point to keep in mind is that while a particular objective may be achievable the objective itself may not be appropriate for you personally.

- Realistic. Since a fitness goal can and should serve as a source of motivation for you, it should be one that is within your reach, yet not too easy to accomplish. A goal that is well beyond your reach can foster a negative attitude towards your exercise program and can diminish your desire to sick with your exercise regimen.

On the other hand, all factors considered, you can be better served if your fitness goals represent a meaningful challenge to you. Such intangibles as "meeting a challenge head on," "pride of accomplishment," "paying the price," etc. can have a positive impact on your efforts to do whatever is necessary to accomplish your fitness goals.

• Timely. A specific date or period of time for achieving your fitness goals should be established. If you have multiple fitness goals, you should identify a schedule that is appropriate for accomplishing each particular goal. From a practical standpoint, you need to be prepared to adjust the time frame for your fitness goals as your circumstances change or as you achieve a clearer understanding of exactly what you can accomplish relative to a specific objective within a given time period.

The process of establishing fitness goals can be further enhanced if you take three additional steps: write your goals down; if you want to pursue an intangible goal, identify measurable indices that can provide you with a reliable indicator of your relative degree of success for that goal; and make sure that your fitness goals are "big enough."

Because each of us tends to remember those things that turn out well for us and either forget or modify those things that are less than we wish they were, you should record your goals in writing. Written goals can serve as a constant reminder and provide you with an effective tracking device to measure the progress of your exercise efforts.

If, for any reason, you want to achieve an intangible objective from your exercise program, you need to establish measurable sub-objectives that might otherwise indicate to you whether your exercise efforts are effective in this regard. For example, if you want to reduce your level of stress by exercising, you might identify what quantifiable "by-products" of stress you could use as evaluative measures for this particular fitness goal (e.g., lessened number and diminished severity of headaches; number of restful hours of sleep attained per night; etc.).

Finally, your fitness goals should be "big enough" to justify your personal commitment of essential resources (time, energy, and money). Obviously, this step mandates that, to the degree possible, you should focus your efforts on reality. Determine what is best for you—not too much," "not too little." In other words, keep your goals in perspective. Be sure they are rooted in a positive, "can do" attitude.

How Can You Prioritize Your Fitness Goals?

When it comes to your exercise program, you have the option of choosing from a wide variety of fitness goals. Obviously, it could be counterproductive and a waste of your time to enumerate too many goals. Furthermore, you need to establish some sort of priority order for those goals.

Each time that you exercise you make a deposit into your 'health bank.'

As with other aspects of the process for establishing fitness goals, you have a great deal of subjective latitude when prioritizing your personal fitness goals. In this regard, a number of factors may be taken into consideration. Do you have an underlying, burning desire to achieve a particular goal? Does a medical/health condition generate a sense of urgency for you to accomplish a specific goal? Are your attitudes and values involved? Is your goal realistic in view of your genetic makeup? Are you satisfying your psychological needs? Does any underlying drive exist in your subconscious?

Frame Your Dreams

The process of establishing appropriate fitness goals is not terribly complicated. The primary attribute you need in this regard is common sense. At a minimum, common sense concerning what you can realistically do either to improve your ability to perform your activities of daily living or to have a positive impact on you level of health. Bear in mind an analogy that can be drawn between setting your goals and framing your dreams. Your fitness goals, as well as your dreams, are like a road map to what you want to accomplish in life. To paraphrase Henry David Thoreau, "In the long run, individuals hit only what they aim at..."

Checking Out the Facts

A very positive and important relationship exists between your fitness level and your health. As a rule, the more fit you are, the more likely you are to be healthy. Accordingly, two of the most valuable steps you can take to enhance your health are to exercise regularly and periodically to evaluate your fitness level to ensure that your exercise efforts are working as planned and in a meaningful way. Each time you exercise, you're making a deposit into your "health bank." Each time you assess your fitness level, you're ensuring that the "health-funds" will be there when you need to draw on them. The benefits of your actions are undeniable.

CHAPTER SIX

DEVELOPING A PERSONALIZED

EXERCISE PROGRAM

In order to make your exercise efforts as productive as possible,
you need to adhere to an exercise prescription that is results-oriented,
time-efficient, and safe.

An ever-increasing amount of information exists concerning the benefits of a physically active lifestyle. This information shows that merely being physically active (e.g., working in the garden, playing with your kids, using the stairs at work instead of an elevator, etc.) can have a substantial effect on how well and how long you live. Considerable evidence also exists that documents the fact that purposeful physical activity (i.e., exercise) can have an even greater impact on your health and longevity.

As such, a strong argument can be made that every individual should exercise on a regular basis. Not only is the value of having everyone engage in a sound exercise program on a regular basis widely acknowledged, the need for individuals to take whatever steps are necessary to ensure that their exercise efforts are as productive as possible is recognized. The primary step in this regard is to identify a prescription for exercising that is results-oriented, time-efficient, and safe.

At You Turn, an exercise prescription is a personalized program of recommended physical activity that is designed to enhance, maintain, or restore your health and fitness levels. Specific guidelines for the intensity, duration, frequency, type, and rate of progression of the exercise program are integral components of a sound exercise prescription.

As a general rule, exercise prescriptions are designed by professionally trained personnel employed at health-club or medical facilities. Regardless of what method you employ to determine what your exercise recipe should be, your exercise program must be based on the following factors: your health and fitness status, the exercise setting, the program's goals, and your personal goals. Once you start your exercise program, you need to periodically assess how well your body is responding to the physical demands you are subjecting it to by exercising. The information you obtain from these assessments can help you to determine whether adjustments in your program's protocol should be considered.

The primary focus of this chapter is to provide an overview of the factors that should be considered in developing a personalized exercise prescription (program) for you. The assumption is that you are both symptom-free and able to engage in routine physical activity without undue cardiovascular or orthopedic risk. If you answered yes to any question on the PAR-Q test in Chapter 4 or there is any reason that you can think of that may result in risk to you by initiating an exercise program (you have seen a doctor recently for any prescription, muscle or joint problem, concern about your general health etc.), you should seek medical approval before starting any exercise program. If you meet these criteria, you can begin a low-intensity exercise program without undergoing exercise testing or a medical examination. In this instance, the only prerequisite is to ensure that your exercise program progresses gradually and that you are alert for and respond appropriately to the development of any unusual physical signs or symptoms.

Once you have determined that exercising will not place you at risk either of being injured or of suffering a serious, program-induced medical condition, your next step is to put your exercise program into action. This step essentially involves addressing the fundamental exercise-related issues of "how much," "how often," "how hard," "what kind," and "where."

You Turn's Recipe for Success

In order to develop an appropriate level of total fitness and to achieve your specific fitness goals, you need an exercise program that addresses the four basic components of health-related fitness—cardiorespiratory fitness, muscular fitness, flexibility, and body composition. The recommended prescription guidelines for developing each of these components are discussed in subsequent chapters. For each component, this information is organized according to the four basic elements of the F.I.T.T. principle: frequency, intensity, time, and type.

Frequency refers to how often you should work out. Intensity addresses how hard you should exercise. Keep in mind that differences exist concerning how hard an individual should exercise when first starting to work out. For example, some people need to exercise at a relatively low level of intensity when they initially begin to train because moderate-intensity exercise is too rigorous for them. Others who are in better condition are able to start exercising at a higher level of intensity. Still others are at a certain age (age 45 in men; age 55 in women) where the intensity level of their initial exercise efforts should be based to a degree on the result of their taking both a medical examination and a supervised maximal or submaximal test.

Time involves how long (duration) you should exercise. Type (mode) explains what kind of exercise addresses a particular exercise-related objective. Because a variety of exercise modalities may address the same fitness component, you need to choose the type of exercise mode that best fits your interests and needs.

You should always remember that the relative success of your exercise efforts will be determined by how well you apply the F.I.T.T. variables to your exercise program, and how well you are able to adhere to certain training principles and guidelines. These training tips and suggestions are discussed in later chapters.

A well-designed exercise program also allows sufficient time for warming up before exercising and cooling down afterwards. It is important to include both of these activities in your overall exercise regimen.

Warm-up and Cool-down Phases

Warm-up and cool-down activities should be included in all exercise programs. Warm up activities prepare your body, especially your cardiovascular and musculoskeletal systems, for the conditioning or stimulus phase of the exercise session. The cool-down phase helps prevent the pooling of blood in your extremities, which reduces the amount of blood to your heart. Light aerobic endurance-type activities, coupled with stretching activities, should provide the fundamental basis for both the warm-up and cool-down phases.

The length of the warm-up and cool-down periods depends on several factors, including the type of activity you engage in during a particular conditioning period, the intensity of the activity, and your age and fitness level. In general, the warm-up and cool-down phases last approximately five to ten minutes each. If you have less time than usual for working out, you should reduce the time allotted for the conditioning phase of your workout, while retaining sufficient time for the warm-up and cool-down phases.

Keeping Things in Perspective

Be aware that some people improve more rapidly than others. For example, if you have led a sedentary lifestyle for years, progress may come more slowly for you than if you had been a habitually active person. Don't be discouraged. Begin exercising at a level that can easily be completed; then gradually increase the amount of work that you perform during a workout. The slower rate of progress is nature's way of minimizing the risk of injury and ensuring appropriate adaptation in muscles previously little-used. Finally, depending on how your body responds to the demands of your exercise program, you need to be both willing and able to modify your exercise prescription as appropriate.

A Prescription for Life

A sound prescription for life involves making sound choices—exercising regularly, eating properly, and avoiding risk factors such as smoking, excessive alcohol consumption, etc. Your optimal health and well-being will be greatly affected by how well you make those choices. Designing, following, and sticking with a personalized exercise program is one of the best lifestyle decisions you'll ever make.

CHAPTER SEVEN

STICKING WITH YOUR

EXERCISE PROGRAM

Your exercise regimen should not only be 'custom-fitted' to your personal needs but also be designed in a way that will encourage you stay with the program on a regular basis.

Your exercise regimen should not only be "custom-fitted" to your personal needs and interests but also be designed in a way that will encourage you to stay with the program on a regular basis. Your willingness and ability to "stay the course" with your exercise efforts is more formally referred to as your level of exercise adherence.

Obviously, without a firm resolve to stick with your exercise program, you can not achieve the benefits of regular exercise. Similarly, funds invested in a savings account will accrue little interest if they are invested only for a few days or weeks. However, giving up on an exercise investment is worse than forsaking a money investment because your level of fitness eventually declines once you stop working out. With finances, the pennies your dollar earns over the short haul are yours to keep.

Why do people drop out of exercise programs? What can be done to increase your level of exercise adherence? Unfortunately, the answers to either question are not clear cut. Just as people join an exercise program for varying reasons, they also drop out because of different factors. A factor that affects one individual may not be important to another person. Without question, the wide array of potentially influential elements contributing to poor exercise adherence serves only to make the task of discovering how to increase your level of adherence to your exercise program even more complicated.

Over the years, attempts have been made to identify those elements that have the greatest impact on exercise adherence. For most people, the four most critical factors with regard to exercise adherence are injuries, time, boredom, and results. Not surprisingly, people don't want to stick with activities that result in discomfort, aches, or injuries. The old adage, "no pain, no gain," simply doesn't make "sense" to most people.

Most individuals also strongly prefer to engage in exercise regimens which are time-efficient. Time is a valuable resource which is not to be expended wastefully. While some individuals may enjoy exercising aerobically for an hour or more, most people simply don't want to devote that kind of time. Fortunately, if developing your level of cardiorespiratory fitness is the primary goal of your workout, you may only need to exercise continuously for as little as 20 minutes to accomplish that particular exercise objective (although the average You Turn workout consists of 30-50 minutes aerobically.

Most of us would prefer to engage in an exercise program that is enjoyable. Boredom has a devastating impact on a person's willingness to stick with a particular activity. At the least, the activity should allow you to disassociate from any negative aspects of the experience and to focus on the positive factors. For example, the "bells and whistles" featured on the consoles of many contemporary exercise machines are designed not only to provide physiological and performance feedback but also to mentally "engage" you in some aspect of the exercise experience other than the physical effort required.

The final primary exercise adherence factor is perhaps the most important of the four—results. As a general rule, most people exercise to enhance their existing level of fitness. Obviously, you are more likely to continue to expend the time and energy involved in exercising if your efforts produce meaningful results. Sooner or later, your results have to warrant your commitment to exercise on a regular basis. Keep in mind that in this regard, it is essential that you're able to identify what results you've actually achieved. As such, you must be able to know where to look for the effects of your exercise efforts either quantitatively or qualitatively (e.g., how many pounds have you lost, are you sleeping better, are you pain free, etc.).

Strategies for Increasing Exercise Adherence

The fundamental basis of any exercise program that wants to maximize the retention level of its participants is that the program must meet the needs of its participants. A number of possible steps may be undertaken to enhance the likelihood that your needs will be met by your exercise regimen.

1. Identify what needs you want to meet by engaging in an exercise program. Do you want to lose weight? How much? Do you need to lower your resting pulse or your blood pressure? Develop a written list of what you need and want your exercise efforts to accomplish. Based upon a thorough evaluation of your list (note: be sure that your identified needs are both honest and attainable), develop a strategy that will enable your needs to be met by your exercise program. Keep in mind that each of your objectives may often be interrelated with one of more of your other training goals—for example, losing weight and developing a "toned-up" look.

2. **Make your program fun. If your exercise program isn't enjoyable, the likelihood that you will stick with it over the long haul is practically nonexistent.** Making a program "fun" may require some degree of ingenuity on your part. The easiest initial step is to choose an exercise activity that you enjoy. If, for example, you hate to jog, it is simply a waste of your time and efforts to run on a regular basis to try to become more fit. Adding variety to your program can also help. Ensuring that the program offers you an opportunity for repeated success is another enjoyment-oriented step. One of the primary keys to achieving a successful experience is to focus on pleasure, not pain, in your exercise program.

3. Make your program as safe as possible. Moderation is the key. Excess in your exercise program's level of intensity, duration, or frequency can lead to an increase in the number and seriousness of musculoskeletal injuries that you experience. More is not always better with regard to exercise. You should make sure you properly use any equipment involved in your exercise regimen. If your exercise program involves the potential of orthopedic trauma (caused by the impact of your feet hitting the floor for example), you should be sure that you exercise in

appropriate footwear. You should also be sensitive to any existing health-risk factors you might have and to the need to make any resultant program modifications that may be necessary. (Note: Refer to Chapter 3 for additional information on health-risk factors.)

4. Make your program as effective as possible. Positive results can have a very positive effect on your commitment to keep expending the effort necessary to engage in your exercise program. The opposite also holds true. The surest way to achieve optimal results from your efforts is to base your exercise regimen on sound exercise principles.

5. Engage in group activities. Research has documented the fact that exercise adherence is lower in programs in which individuals work out by themselves than in those which incorporate group dynamics. For a number of interrelated factors (which vary from program to program and individual to individual), the social reinforcement, camaraderie, and companionship associated with a group program tend to facilitate a higher level of exercise compliance.

6. Set personal program goals and periodically assess to what degree your goals are being met. Your personal goals should be mutually developed in consultation between you and any certified fitness professional from whom you may solicit advice. Your goals should be challenging, yet realistic. From time to time, you should also assess whether or not your exercise program is working. Periodically evaluating the progress you attain from your exercise program can serve several purposes. First, it can enable you to determine how effective the program is and whether any adjustments need to be made. Second, your physiological or performance results can be used to develop the equivalent of a "report card" to provide you with additional positive reinforcement.

7. Make your program convenient and comfortable. You should schedule your exercise program at a time most well-matched to your schedule of availability (e.g., before work; after work; during the day; etc.). In addition, the area in which you exercise should reflect a user-friendly philosophy. At a minimum, it should be very clean and bright. By the same token, whenever possible, you might consider working out to music. Research has shown that appropriate background music in an exercise area can play a positive role by masking any fatigue you might experience and stimulating you to work out more energetically.

8. Solicit support for your program from a close friend or a significant other. Your ability to stick with your exercise program is often strongly influenced by how those closest to you feel about your involvement with the program. Accordingly, if feasible, you should get someone to exercise with you on a regular basis. Their involvement and/or support can help you weather any feelings that might arise that might make you want to skip a workout or two…or more.

Sticking with your Commitment

The important thing to keep in mind with regard to exercising is to ask yourself a very pointed question: "If you know what to do, why aren't you doing it?" Your answer to that inquiry can help you deal with any reluctance you may have to stick with your decision to exercise regularly. Keep in mind that whatever "price" you may have to pay to exercise on a regular basis (i.e., time, money, effort, etc.) is relatively small when you consider the "price" exacted by a sedentary lifestyle. At a minimum, the true cost of not exercising involves placing your health at risk. What better reason could you have to stick with your commitment to exercise?

CHAPTER EIGHT

DEVELOPING

CARDIORESPIRATORY FITNESS

When exercising be smart…heart smart.

The appropriate prescription criteria for developing cardiorespiratory fitness is fairly well-defined. Most professionals in the exercise science and medical communities recommend following the guidelines developed by the American College of Sports Medicine (ACSM). ACSM's specific guidelines for developing and maintaining cardiorespiratory fitness in a healthy adult are presented in Table 8-1. In addition to providing information concerning the four F.I.T.T. prescription variables, ACSM's guidelines also address the appropriate rate of progression for developing this particular component of fitness.

- Frequency of training. Three to five days per week.

- Intensity. Either 50 to 85 percent of maximal oxygen uptake (VO2 max) or 60 to 90 percent of maximal heart rate. It should also be noted that exercise of a relatively low- to - moderate intensity may provide important health benefits and may result in increased fitness in some individuals (i.e., those who were previously sedentary and low in fitness).

- Duration of training. Twenty to 60 minutes of continuous aerobic activity. The actual amount of time that should be spent in aerobic exercise generally depends on the relative intensity of the activity. For example, activities involving a lower intensity should be conducted over a longer period of time. The emphasis should be placed on the total amount of work performed, which can be estimated by the caloric expenditure associated with the activity.

- Mode of activity. An appropriate modality for developing cardiorespiratory fitness is any activity that meets the following criteria: one that uses your body's large muscle groups, can be maintained continuously, and is rhythmic and aerobic in nature (e.g., running, jogging, walking, stair stepping, swimming, skating, bicycling, rowing, cross-country skiing, and various endurance game activities). In the beginning sessions of an exercise program, low-impact activities such as walking, cycling, and mechanical stair stepping are recommended because of the low level of orthopedic stress they place on your body.

- Rate of progression. In most instances, the ability of your body to adapt to the stresses imposed upon it (sometimes referred to as the training effect) allows you over time to increase gradually the total amount of work you can do. In exercise performed in a continuous (non-stop) manner, increasing the amount of work performed can be achieved by increasing either the intensity of the exercise or the duration of the exercise bout, or by some combination of the two. The most significant conditioning effects are typically observed during the first six to eight weeks of an exercise program. An individual's exercise prescription is normally adjusted as these conditioning effects occur. The degree of adjustment depends on the individual involved, additional feedback from periodic assessments, and/or the exercise performance of the individual during the exercise sessions.

Table 8-1. ASCM guidelines for developing and maintaining cardiorespiratory fitness in an healthy adult.

Frequency of Exercise Sessions

Frequency of exercise refers to the number of exercise sessions per week. While some evidence exists that shows that you can improve your level of cardiorespiratory fitness with an exercise frequency of less than three days per week, such improvements tend to be minimal. It appears that your body responds best to three to five days per week of moderate-intensity aerobic exercise, with sessions lasting 20 to 60 minutes. Accordingly, the traditional recommendation of a "work-one-day and rest-one-day" routine remains a valid approach if you want to improve your level of cardiorespiratory fitness.

It appears that your body responds best to three to five days per week of moderate-intensity aerobic exercise, with sessions lasting 20 to 30 minutes.

It should be pointed out that if, prior to starting to exercise, you led a relatively sedentary lifestyle, the frequency of your exercise program should initially be established at three days per week. Fewer than three sessions per week would not provide a sufficient training stimulus for significant improvement to occur. On the other hand, engaging in additional sessions might place you at undue risk for orthopedic injuries and expose you to an exercise environment that might have a negative effect on your level of exercise adherence. If you want to increase the frequency of your training bouts, you should do so gradually, depending on your age, initial and existing fitness status, personal needs and interests, and exercise objectives.

Intensity of Exercise

Perhaps the most important component of an exercise prescription is the level of exercise intensity. The prescribed level of intensity must be sufficient to tax your cardiovascular system, but not so severe that it exceeds your cardiovascular system's capability to adapt to the stresses that you impose on it. If you are an apparently healthy individual who wants to develop and maintain cardiorespiratory fitness, the ACSM recommends that the intensity of your exercise regimen be between either 50 and 85 percent of your maximum oxygen uptake capacity (VO2 max) or 60 to 90% of your computed maximal heart-rate.

It is generally accepted, however, that an appropriate intensity threshold for achieving a training effect is at the low end of this continuum for those who have been sedentary, and at the high end of the scale for those who have been physically active. Exercise intensity can be monitored simply by measuring the rate at which your heart beats during exercise or by subjectively rating the level of physical exertion using the Perceived Exertion (RPE) scale shown in Table 8-2.

Determining Exercise Intensity by Target Heart-Rate

How fast your heart should beat during exercise depends on your age and fitness level. If you are just starting a training program, you should exercise at the lower end of the intensity range (i.e., 50 to 70% of your maximal heart rate). You can estimate your maximal heart rate by taking the number 220 and subtracting your age (220-age=max heart rate predicted). While this is a universally accepted estimate of maximal heart rate it can vary +/- 15 beats per minute. This means if your actual maximal heart rate is 180, the estimate could be as low as 165 and as high as 195. Obviously, this range of prediction is not ideal. At You Turn, we conduct a monitored exercise evaluation and monitor heart rate response to a known intensity as this is a more precisely measure of your heart rate response to exercise. When your heart rate response is lower than prescribed for a particular exercise intensity (usually after three to six months), you should gradually increase your exercise intensity level until you reach the middle of the training range of your maximal heart rate (i.e., 70 to 80%). As your level of aerobic

Borg Ratings of Perceived Exertion (RPE)		
RPE		**Newer Rating Scale**
6		0 Nothing at all
7 Very, very light		0.5 Very, very weak
8		1 Very weak
9 Very light		2 Weak
10		3 Moderate
11 Fairly light		4 Somewhat strong
12		5 Strong
13 Somewhat hard		6
14		7 Very strong
15 Hard		8
16		9
17 Very hard		10 Very, very strong
18		Maximal
19 Very, very hard		
20		

Table 8-2.

fitness continues to improve, you should adjust the exercise intensity toward the higher end of the range (i.e., 80 to 90%).

You should avoid exercising above your target heart-rate range, because such a practice could place you at greater risk of injury. As a general rule, if you are unable to comfortably carry on a conversation while exercising (i.e. the "talk test"), you should reduce your exercise intensity regardless of your heart-rate response. The "talk test" tends to err on the side of conservatism and can be very helpful in ensuring that the intensity of your exercise bout is not excessive.

To measure your training heart-rate during exercise, you should stop approximately every 5 to 10 minutes during your workout and count your pulse (i.e., heart rate monitor). Your pulse rate is normally counted by palpating your carotid artery. To take your pulse rate, you should place your middle and index fingers below your jaw line in the groove adjacent to your Adam's apple. Gentle pressure should be applied, because when excessive pressure is applied to the carotid artery, your heart-rate will slow down. As a result, your count will not accurately reflect the exercise intensity of your workout. In fact, you could pass out. To avoid such a risk, your heart rate can also be measured by palpating the radial artery on the thumb side of your wrist.

When taking your pulse during exercise, you should count for 10 seconds, and then multiply by six. If your pulse rate is below an appropriate target range, you should gradually increase your level of exercise intensity. In turn, however, if your pulse rate exceeds the upper end of an appropriate target heart-rate range, the intensity of your exercise bout should be decreased.

Determining Exercise Intensity by RPE

Your exercise intensity can also be monitored by rating your level of perceived exertion during a particular exercise bout using the Borg RPE scale. Available evidence suggests that RPE (rating of perceived exertion), like your heart rate, can be effectively used to prescribe and monitor exercise intensity. For example, regularly exercising at an RPE of "somewhat hard or strong" has been shown to significantly improve aerobic capacity. When exercising at a "somewhat hard" level, you typically are able to pass the "talk test" and engage in the activity for a sustained period of time. When exercising at a "very hard" level, however, your heart rate tends to be relatively high. As a result, it is difficult for you to talk during the activity or to exercise for an extended period of time.

Duration (Time) of the Exercise Session

The duration of exercise refers to the amount of time working out (in minutes) at which you should maintain the proper intensity level. Typically, a conditioning phase lasts for at least 20 to 30 minutes, which corresponds to the amount of time required for the improvement or maintenance of functional capacity. If you are just beginning an exercise program, you should start with approximately 10 to 20 minutes of aerobic activity. On the other hand, if you are in "average" condition, you can exercise for a longer period of time (i.e., 20-30 minutes). It should be kept in mind that the optimum duration of an exercise session usually depends on the intensity of your workout. More importantly, in order to achieve health and fitness benefits, the time you spend exercising should be long enough to at least expend approximately 300 calories.

Mode (Type) of Cardiorespiratory Exercise

Your aerobic activities should be selected based on your functional capacity, interest, time, personal goals, and objectives. A fitness program usually starts with easily quantifiable activities, such as walking, exercise cycling, or stair stepping, so that the proper exercise intensity can be determined and achieved. When exercising three to four days a week for 30 to 40 minutes a day at the appropriate intensity, any activity utilizing your large muscle groups can be incorporated into an exercise program designed to enhance your level of cardiorespiratory fitness.

The ACSM differentiates between several types of cardiorespiratory endurance activities. Activities such as walking, jogging, stair climbing, or cycling can be easily maintained at a constant intensity. The variability between individuals in terms of energy expenditure is relatively low in these types of activities. Activities, such as swimming or cross-country skiing, the rate of energy expenditure is strongly related to your skill or proficiency at the activity. Although the level of intensity involved in these activities tends to vary between individuals, you can maintain a relatively constant intensity while engaging in this type of activity. On the other hand, activities such as tennis, basketball, racquetball, etc. by their very nature, are highly variable in intensity both between individuals and within a specific individual.

The types of activities recommended by a professional or chosen by you will directly depend on the results of your health-risk assessment and your current fitness level. For example, high intensity activities are generally not prescribed for previously sedentary, at-risk, or diseased individuals, because such activities can vary a great deal in intensity.

Rate of Progression

The recommended rate of progression in an aerobic exercise program depends on several interrelated factors, including your fitness status, health status, age, needs or goals, and support provided by your friends and family. The ACSM defines three distinct stages of an exercise prescription:

1. Initial Conditioning Stage. This stage typically lasts four to six weeks, but may be longer depending on your body's adaptation to the exercise program. Your exercise prescription will generally range from 40 to 85 % (50 to 90% of your maximal heart-rate) of your aerobic capacity. In order to avoid undue muscle soreness, injury, discomfort, and discouragement, at You Turn your exercise level may be slightly lower than 40% of aerobic capacity depending upon your entry level of fitness and physician recommendations if any.

2. Improvement Conditioning Stage. This stage normally lasts 12 to 20 weeks, and is the period during which your exercise progression is the most rapid. For example, the intensity of your exercise bout is increased to 50 to 85% of your VO2 max (or 60 to 90% of your maximal heart-rate), while the duration of your exercise session is increased as frequently as every two to three weeks. The frequency and magnitude of these progressive increments are dictated by the rate at which adaptation to your conditioning program occurs.

3. Maintenance Conditioning Stage. When your desired level of conditioning is attained, the maintenance stage begins—usually after the first six months of training. At this time, your emphasis is often refocused from an exercise program primarily involving fitness activities to one that includes a more diverse array of enjoyable physical activities.

Systems of Cardiorespiratory Training

Several systems of cardiorespiratory training exist. These systems can be employed to achieve several objectives, including add variety to your program, offer a degree of cross-training to your aerobic exercise training efforts, or provide a means to vary the intensity level of your exercise regimen. Four of the most commonly employed systems are continuous training, interval training, Fartlek training, and circuit training.

- Continuous training. This system involves exercising in a continuous manner in modalities like jogging, cycling, swimming, or walking at a prescribed level of intensity without rest intervals. Typically, your level of intensity is relatively consistent throughout your workout.

- Interval training. This system involves a repeated series of exercise bouts interspersed with rest periods. Higher intensity levels can be incorporated during particular bouts to further overload your cardiorespiratory system because of your opportunity to rest periodically. As a rule, you should not perform more than one or two interval training workouts per week.

- Fartlek training. This system involves a free form of training where you base your exercise-rest cycle on how you feel during the workout (e.g., exercise hard for "x" number of seconds or distance; rest for "x" number of seconds; etc.).

- Circuit training. This system involves having you exercise through a series of exercise stations, performing a prescribed number of exercises. Sometimes, one or more types of fitness exercises are interspersed in the circuit to develop several components of fitness simultaneously (i.e., cardiorespiratory fitness and muscular fitness).

Record Keeping

At You Turn, we believe that recording what you do and how well you do it on a daily basis is one of the keys to success. While at a You Turn facility, your entire program is monitored with a computerized key that records all weights, repetitions and the quality of the exercise conducted. With this information, your personal lifestyle coach can review your training and make recommendations for continued progress. When outside the You Turn center, record what training you performed during every workout: what exercises you did and in what order you did them.

Heart Smart

If you want to develop total fitness and in the process achieve the boundless benefits of exercise, there are certain rules to which you must strictly adhere. Accordingly, if you want to be aerobically fit—and you should—you need to learn the "prescription rules" for developing cardiorespiratory fitness and implement them as an integral part of your regular conditioning routine. In other words, you need to undertake a systematic, ordered approach to ensuring that your heart-lung complex is in optimal shape, just as you would for any other critical task in your life. As the familiar song goes… "You gotta have heart." Quite simply, be smart… heart smart. Your health demands it, and your body deserves it.

CHAPTER NINE

DEVELOPING

MUSCULAR FITNESS

Virtually everyone—young or old, male or female—can experience
improvements in muscular fitness.

The purpose of this chapter on muscular fitness is not to show every type of exercise or movement that can be utilized to improve muscular strength and endurance. Frankly, there are many opposing philosophies on how to train a muscle and a thousand books that are written explaining each and everyone. At You Turn, we want you to understand why it is important to develop muscular fitness at all ages and how the muscle adapts to your exercise. We feel if you have the basics down, you can apply them to any one of the numerous strategies available.

If you want to have stronger more durable muscles and bones, improve your physical appearance, and enhance your self-image, then you need to perform resistance exercise (strength training). Fortunately, virtually everyone—young or old, male or female—can experience improvements in muscular fitness. The first step you need to take to improve your level of muscular fitness (muscular strength and muscular endurance) is to decide that you will do whatever it reasonably takes to become muscularly fit.

Any attempt you make to increase your level of muscular fitness may be somewhat unproductive, however, if you do not adhere to proper techniques and training methods. Sensible training methods, combined with the necessary desire and effort, will lead to optimal improvement in your level of muscular fitness. One without the other is an unwise and ineffective approach.

Getting Started

Once you make up your mind to strength train, you're on your way to an improved level of muscular fitness. Despite its numerous advantages, however, strength training can often seem very complicated. Any confusion you may have in this regard can be cleared up if you have the facts—facts about the myths surrounding strength training, facts that can help you set realistic goals for your strength training efforts, facts that can enable you to design a resistance exercise program to meet those goals, and facts that can put you into position to enjoy the benefits of your efforts.

The Benefits of Strength Training

Strength training offers numerous benefits. Simply stated, strength training can meet the needs and interests of a wide variety of people. Among the primary benefits of strength training are the following:

- Improves your ability to perform the activities of daily living—at home, work, or play. As a result, you'll be better able to maintain a physically active and relatively challenging lifestyle. One of the cornerstones of independent living is having enough muscular fitness to be able to perform your daily tasks (from climbing stairs at work to lifting heavy materials at home).

- Enriches your physical health. A higher level of muscular fitness can greatly reduce your chances of suffering either muscle-related or skeletal injuries. It's estimated that approximately half of the various injuries that occur in physical activity could be prevented through higher levels of muscular fitness. Strength training can also help individuals who suffer from a particular medical condition or physical problem. For example, strength training improves the upper body muscular fitness of cardiac patients whose muscles have lost tone and function due to physical inactivity. Strength training performed over an extended period of time can also increase the density of your bones - an action that helps to lover your risk of osteoporosis. In addition, strength training helps provide pain relief to people with osteoarthritic conditions by reducing the stress their joints must handle. Finally, strength training appears to play an important role in treating and preventing lower back pain.

- Uplifts your mental health. Having a higher level of muscular fitness can improve how you feel about yourself. As your self-esteem rises, your outlook on other factors in your life will tend to improve also. Strength training on a regular basis can also affect you in other positive ways, including helping you better control and manage stress and improving both the quality and the quantity of your sleep.

- Enhances your appearance. Strength training can provide you with readily apparent feedback on your exercise efforts. Substantial changes in your strength level and the tone of your muscles can occur over a relatively brief period of time. The fit, healthy look is generally a matter of muscle tone, and muscle tone is a by-product of proper strength training.

Common Myths About Strength Training

Your attitudes toward strength training could also be clouded by one or more of the many misconceptions surrounding strength training. Among the more common myths about strength training are the following:

- Myth: Lifting weights will cause you to develop large, bulky muscles. Not true. Most people (i.e., less than 20% of men and 1% of women) don't have the genetic potential to develop large muscles because they don't have enough testosterone—a hormone needed for the development of muscle bulk.

- Myth: Strength training makes you muscle-bound. Muscle-bound is a term that connotes a lack of flexibility. However, proper strength training doesn't make you less flexible, it makes you more flexible. If you keep your muscles loose and supple by regularly going through a full range of motion (a requirement of proper strength training), you will stay flexible.

- Myth: More is better. With any form of exercise you eventually reach a point of either diminishing or no returns. You take a chance of injuring yourself if you don't use common sense to decide "how much is enough." The quality of your strength training is much more important than the quantity of time you spend lifting. As a point of fact, a quality workout of 30 minutes can effectively and safely develop muscular fitness.

- Myth: Women can't get strong. Women can and should develop muscular fitness. Women have a potential for muscular fitness—particularly in their upper bodies—that often remains untapped. In fact, the "average woman" gains strength at a slightly faster rate than the "average man".

- Myth: Strength training defeminizes women. The potential functional, health, mental, and physical benefits of strength training must not be confined to members of the male domain. Regardless of your gender, proper strength training—by helping you increase your physical working capacity, improve your body composition, and lower your risk of injury—will make you look and feel better. In reality, tight, firm muscles have nothing to do with the objectionable and patronizing term, defeminizing.

- Myth: No pain, no gain. A sensible strength training program might be uncomfortable, but it should not be painful. It should put a reasonable demand on your muscles to increase your strength, without exposing you to an unreasonable risk of injury.

- Myth: Muscles turn to fat when you stop training. Muscles cannot turn into fat. They don't have the physiological ability to change from one type of tissue to another. On the other hand, muscles exhibit the property of "use it or lose it". If you don't use a muscle, it will literally waste (atrophy) away. When someone has a cast removed from a leg that had been broken, the unused leg muscles look smaller than they were before the injury. If muscle turned to fat, you would see a "fat ball" when the cast was removed, not atrophied leg muscles.

- Myth: You must take protein supplements to get a fit physique. Your muscular fitness is not enhanced by using protein supplements because your body can't store extra protein. Excess protein is not used to build muscle tissue. It is converted to fat and stored. As such, if you consume extra protein in addition to your regular diet, any weight gain will probably be fat. Excess protein also can lead to dehydration and loss of urinary calcium. Chronic calcium loss from too much protein increases the risk of osteoporosis, especially in women.

- Myth: Proper strength training must be complex. The simpler your approach to strength training, the more likely your efforts will be successful. Making your strength training program too technical can be counterproductive. For example, it can be confusing and can compromise your strength training efforts or can increase the possibility that you won't stick with your training program. Basic muscular development programs—those emphasizing effectiveness, efficiency, and safety over complexity—usually produce the best results.

- Myth: Proper strength training is expensive. Muscles respond to the stress applied to them. Other factors being equal, muscles can't discern between 50 lbs of stress on an inexpensive barbell from 50 lbs of stress on a high-tech machine costing thousands of dollars. In reality, your strength training program doesn't even have to involve equipment to be effective.

- Myth: Strength training is a contest. Individuals who focus on competition in strength training tend to injure themselves or get discouraged and drop out of their programs. It is unrealistic to compare your training numbers (particularly the amount lifted on a specific exercise) with those of other participants. How much you can lift is a by-product of several factors, most of which you have no control over (e.g., the length of your arms or legs). As trite as it may sound, the adage, "do your best and leave the rest," should govern your efforts to develop muscular fitness.

- Myth: Strength training is for young people. It's never too late to improve the quality of your life by enjoying a higher level of muscular fitness. Muscular fitness can extend your functional life span. In fact, individuals in their 90s have improved their levels of muscular fitness and have enhanced their quality of life by participating in strength training programs.

- Myth: You'll have a greater need for vitamins. The vitamin needs of an active person are generally no greater than those of a sedentary one. Vitamins do not contribute significantly to your body structure and do not provide you with a direct source of body energy. Accordingly, physically active people receive little or no benefit from taking vitamin supplements if they eat a balanced diet. If you eat a variety of healthful foods (breads, cereals, grains, fruits, vegetables, lean meats, etc.), your intake of vitamins will be adequate. On the other hand, if you don't have the opportunity to consume a healthy diet on a regular basis, nutritional supplements may fill an appropriate role for you.

- Myth: Rigorous strength training rids your body of fat. While strength training can firm and tone your muscles, it does not burn away fat. Keep in mind that some fat is needed for normal bodily functions, such as activity in the brain, nerve tissue, heart, bone marrow, and cell membranes.

- Myth: Strength training can't be fun. Strength training can and should be enjoyable. You can design a strength training program that both meets your physical needs and is fun. Remember, staying with your exercise program is more likely when you enjoy what you're doing.

Identifying Which Goals Are Right For You

Before you begin strength training regularly, you should take stock of your personal needs. Ask yourself, "Why do I want to strength train?" The answer can help you decide how to train and what program to follow. You may want to strengthen your body for a specific sport, or supplement a weight-loss program by using strength training to firm up. One of your primary goals should be to be able to handle your body weight when doing calisthenic-type exercises such as push-ups, chin-ups, and dips. Being able to handle your body weight shows that you can use your muscles functionally. Keep in perspective that the life-enhancing applications of doing a 200-lb bench press, for example, are limited.

Organizing Your Strength Training Program

Once you've identified your strength training goals, the next step is to design a program to meet them. Designing a strength training program involves seven variables:

- Selecting your exercises
- Ordering your exercises
- Determining repetitions/set
- Determining number of sets/exercise
- Determining weight
- Limiting the time between exercises
- Allowing rest and recovery time between your workouts

Selecting Your Exercises

As a rule of thumb, you should limit your strength training workout to 12 to 14 exercises. Doing more than 14 exercises is counterproductive physiologically and psychologically. You reach a point where additional work is simply not worth the effort. Your workout should include about 10 exercises that will develop the major muscle groups in your body (lower back and buttocks, legs, chest, shoulders, arms, and abdominals) plus 2 to 4 exercises chosen to meet your particular needs or interests. For example, if you're prone to groin pulls, you'll want to include exercises that develop your inner thigh muscles. If you're a tennis player, you may want to include exercises for your forearms—the gripping muscles.

Ordering Your Exercises

Your strength training program should begin with exercises using your largest muscles and move to those using your smallest muscles. Most strength training exercises are designed to develop the largest muscle involved in the exercise. If you stop an exercise because a smaller muscle has become fatigued before a larger one, then you've compromised the possible gains for the larger muscle. For example, if you start your workout with modified sit-ups, you'll fatigue your abdominal muscles—muscles that should be exercised last. A problem then occurs when you perform an exercise (such as a squat) in which your abdominals act as stabilizers. You have to either lift less weight during the exercise (thereby decreasing your need for stabilization), or subject yourself to risk of injury (by exercising at a level of intensity that your abdominals can't safely support). Either way, you may lose.

Determining Repetitions, Sets, and Weight

These three variables are the numbers crunch of strength training. A repetition is doing a specific exercise one time. A set is doing a particular number of repetitions in a row, before stopping. The weight used is the level of resistance (demand) that you put on your muscles while exercising. You have many choices about how to structure your repetitions, sets, and weight. Two of the most commonly employed methods are: the multiple- and single-set approaches.

Multiple-set approach. This approach to strength training suggests that you:

- complete three sets of 5 to 8 repetitions for developing strength,
- complete three sets of 9 to 15 repetitions for developing endurance.

When taking the multiple-set approach, you should use a weight that will enable you to do all sets somewhere between the minimum and maximum number of repetitions before reaching muscle failure (inability to complete a repetition). Alternatively, select a weight based on the "one-max rep system" by determining the maximum amount you can lift in one repetition of an exercise, and then lift an arbitrary percentage (usually between 50-75%) of that amount on each set of the exercise.

Single-set approach. Another popular approach to strength training is high intensity training (H.I.T). H.I.T. proponents believe that "more is not better." They claim that once you work your muscles to their capacity, additional work is a waste of time and possibly counterproductive. H.I.T. involves performing one set of 8 to 12 repetitions until you reach muscle failure, whether you're developing strength or endurance. In other words, you should lift a weight that will let you do at least 8, but not more than 12, repetitions of the exercise. You should increase the amount you lift during a particular exercise only when you can do 12 repetitions of that exercise. If you can't do 8 repetitions at the increased weight, you've either increased the weight too much or raised your resistance level too soon.

Individuals who support the H.I.T. approach believe that most people don't have a constant maximum strength. Your mental state can greatly affect how much you can lift. If you're "up", you often feel like you can lift the world. If you're "down", you may feel like every weight is attached to a grand piano. Unfortunately, it is sometimes difficult to determine what mental state you're in. If you do your best on every exercise and follow sound training guidelines, you'll achieve whatever results are genetically possible.

Limiting the Time Between Exercises

You should limit the time between exercises to less than one minute to make the most of your time in the weight room. No science involved here, just sound time management. Minimize your standing around. Get in and get out without chaos or wasted time. Minimizing the time between exercises helps you focus on maximum effort while you're training.

Allowing Time Between Your Workouts

Unless you are doing a split routine workout (upper body exercises one day, lower body exercises the next day), you should allow at least one full day between your workouts. An alternate-day schedule (Monday-Wednesday-Friday or Tuesday-Thursday-Saturday) is the most commonly followed system. As you get older, you generally need more rest between workouts. Accordingly, you may want to occasionally give yourself two full days of rest between workouts instead of one.

Assessing Your Strength

Once you have your strength training plan it's time to get a "status report" about your level of strength and endurance. Assessing your level of muscular fitness can help you determine where to begin your strength program and what deficiencies you might have, such as weak abdominals, a low level of upper body strength, or a muscular imbalance (e.g., strong quadriceps and weak hamstrings). Your training program can then be tailored to take care of these issues.

Strength Training Principles

You should become familiar with the essential training principles to make sure you get the most out of your strength training workouts. In this regard, among the more critical factors are intensity, specifications, progression, and recovery time.

Intensity

A muscle becomes stronger when a demand is placed on it. If you place less demand on your muscles than your muscles can handle, you'll get less improvement than you are capable of achieving. For example, if you do a biceps curl set using a 10-lb dumbbell for six consecutive workouts, you won't get as much improvement as if you had increased your weight to 12 or 15 lbs after the third workout - making your workout more intense. Considerable debate exists about what level of intensity you need to achieve maximum results. One theory suggests that anything less than an all-out effort will produce less than maximum gains. Another theory suggests that an appropriate demand is achieved by training at a predetermined percentage of your maximum level of strength for each exercise. Depending on your philosophy, the percentage may change from set to set and from exercise to exercise.

Specificity

Only one proper way exists to perform a specific exercise, and you should emphasize correct technique when strength training. If you compromise the mechanics for doing a particular exercise, you will compromise the results you achieve by performing that exercise. As such, you should learn how to do each exercise, and then do each one correctly. Keep in mind that how you do an exercise is much more important than how much weight you lift. One of the most effective ways to make sure you use the proper techniques is to work out with a training partner who knows how to perform the exercise and who has the temperament to help you train correctly.

Progression

Your strength training program should be progressive in nature. Too much, too soon will lead either to an injury or failure, or both. You should gradually increase the stress you place on your muscles as they are able to meet the imposed demand. As your muscles adapt to a point where they can handle the stresses imposed on them (by getting stronger), you should gradually increase the resistance level to stimulate new growth and development.

Recovery Time

When you stress a muscle beyond what it can normally handle, some rest is needed for the muscle tissues, tendons, and ligaments to recover. If the time between exercise sessions is too brief, your muscle may be unable to make the adaptations needed before being stressed again. In this instance, the muscle either will not develop to the extent possible or may suffer a decrease in strength. Conversely, if you take too much time between workouts, your muscles will gradually return to their untrained level.

Minimizing Injury, Maximizing Results

Doing your strength training exercises properly will enable you to achieve results more efficiently and safely. Properly performing strength training exercises involves several considerations, including muscle balance, full range of motion, speed of movement, and safety issues.

Muscle Balance

Your body has muscles that oppose each other—your quadriceps muscles (front thigh) are opposed by your hamstring muscles (rear thigh). If one is too strong for the other, you risk injury to the weaker muscle. Pairs of opposing muscles should have about a 1:1 strength relationship. The exception is your quadriceps and hamstrings, which should be 3:2 (your quadriceps should be about 150% stronger than your hamstrings). For maximum results, alternate pushing exercises with pulling exercises (e.g., do a leg press, then a leg curl).

Full Range of Motion

Every exercise should be done through a full range of motion (the degree to which there is normal movement around a joint). If you don't go through a full range of motion, you will perform less work and will eventually decrease your level of flexibility in the joints involved in the exercise.

Speed of Movement

Do every exercise at a controlled speed. If you raise and lower a weight slowly (about two seconds on the lifting phase and four seconds on the lowering phase), your muscles will do effective work throughout the exercise. If you throw or jerk the weight, your muscles will be working only at the beginning and at the end of the lift. No work will be done in the midrange of the lift. In addition, the rapid deceleration in throwing a weight increases your chances of being injured.

Safety Issues

Among the factors involved in resistance training, none is more important than safety. In addition to using the proper lifting techniques you should adhere to the following safety principles: warm up properly, handle muscle soreness effectively, use well-trained spotters, breathe properly, wear appropriate clothing, and use correct grip positions. If you adhere to these guidelines and use common sense, strength training is a relatively safe activity.

Warming up. Common sense suggests that you spend a few minutes before strength training to prepare for the demands of rigorous activity. Warming up serves several purposes. The primary purpose is to slowly elevate your pulse to an aerobic level, thereby increasing your cardiac output. As a result, your body and muscle temperature is raised. This increases the activity of the enzymes in your working skeletal muscles, which increases the metabolism of those muscles. The viscosity in the muscle is reduced, and muscle blood flow is increased. Therefore more oxygen and fuel reach the muscles involved in the activity.

A proper warm-up also improves the mechanical efficiency and power of the working muscles. Furthermore, the time necessary to transmit nervous impulses is improved, augmenting your reaction time and coordination. Warming up decreases the likelihood of injuries to your muscles and the supporting connective tissues involved in the activity. The increase in temperature and blood flow to these muscles and supporting tissues is particularly beneficial if you are doing high-power, explosive-type exercises.

A warm-up session should be at least five minutes, raise the core temperature of your body (signaled by the fact that you perspire), and involve your major joints. A typical warm-up session might include running in place for a minute and then doing a set of strength exercises using very light resistance.

Muscle Soreness. There are several different theories about the cause of muscle soreness that persists for two or three days after an unusually hard strength training workout. The most widely accepted theory is that muscle soreness results from microtears to the muscle and its tendinous attachments. Usually this damage occurs during the beginning of a program when the relatively understressed muscle fibers haven't adapted to the new demands imposed on them. Soreness also can occur when you dramatically increase the intensity of your training or incorporate new exercises into your workout.

Spotters. When you are not using progressive resistance training machines with built in spotting mechanisms, spotters help you while you are doing resistance training. Their assistance can take many forms. For an example, one of their responsibilities is to ensure that you are not injured by having a weight fall on you. If you can't complete a repetition, your spotter will take the weight from you (if asked). Spotters can also get help if you are injured while training. Another purpose of spotters is to give you constant verbal feedback—either to motivate you or to ensure that you use the proper techniques. Spotters can help you bring a heavy weight into the starting position for an exercise (particularly for negative-only training). Remember, anyone with the responsibility of spotting must know the proper techniques for doing the exercises that are being performed.

Breathing. Never hold your breath while strength training. Hold your breath while exerting force can cause a dangerous buildup of inner-thoracic pressure. The pressure inside your rib cage compresses the right side of your heart. This action restricts the flow of blood and, consequently, oxygen to your entire body (a process called the "Valsalva maneuver"). Two theories are generally advocated concerning the proper approach to breathing while strength training. The simplest and most sensible guideline suggests that you should breathe normally and regularly as you train. A second and more involved theory contends that you should control your breathing pattern while you exercise. Proponents of this theory recommend that you inhale during the negative (lowering) phase of the exercise and exhale during the positive (lifting) phase of the exercise.

Fine-Tuning Your Efforts

As you progress through your strength training program, you will notice many changes in how you look, feel, and perform. You also might notice that, although you've been working out consistently, a particular muscle has reached its peak—you just can't seem to lift more weight. Maybe you'll find that you're not as interested in strength training as you used to be, or that your muscles are getting unusually sore. Conversely, perhaps you've "caught fire" and want to lift for power or for competition. As such, you need to deal effectively with the issues of strength plateaus, overtraining, and detraining.

Strength Plateaus

During a strength plateau, further gains in strength in a muscle or muscle group have temporarily halted. For whatever reason, you can't make progress on a particular exercise; you can't handle more resistance. Normally a plateau doesn't occur in all muscle groups at the same time. If you're stuck for more than a few consecutive workouts, you can use one or more of the following techniques for overcoming a strength plateau:

- Include different exercises in your program.
- Change the frequency of your training.
- Change the number of sets you perform.
- Modify your exercise—do more repetitions with less resistance or fewer repetitions with more resistance.
- Increase the intensity level of your workouts.

Overtraining

You should design your program so that it gives enough training stimulus for positive physiological changes to occur without going beyond your abilities. Overtraining occurs when there is an imbalance between training and recovery. The symptoms of overtraining vary from one person to another. The most common signs of overtraining frequently involve one or more of the following:

- Chronic muscle or joint soreness
- Increased incidence of musculoskeletal injuries
- Impaired physical performance
- Reduced enthusiasm and desire for training

- Increased resting heart rate (your heart rate taken first thing in the morning, before rising out of bed)
- Increased resting blood pressure
- Increased incidence of colds and infections
- Impaired recovery from exercise (you remain highly fatigued well after you finish your workout)
- Increased perceived exertion during your normal workouts
- Reduced appetite
- Undue weight loss
- Disturbed sleep patterns
- Increased depression, irritability, or anxiety

Detraining

Detraining occurs when you cease or reduce your training efforts. This factor can lead to losses in strength and other benefits you may have achieved in a strength training program. To maintain gains in strength, the intensity of demand on your muscles must be kept at least at the existing program levels. However, you can reduce the volume and frequency of your training without appreciably affecting your level of strength.

Record Keeping

At You Turn, we believe that recording what you do and how well you do it on a daily basis is one of the keys to success. While at a You Turn facility, your entire program is monitored with a computerized key that records all weights, repetitions and the quality of the exercise conducted. With this information, your personal lifestyle coach can review your training and make recommendations for continued progress. When outside the You Turn center, record what training you performed during every workout: what exercises you did, in what order you did them, how many sets and reps of each you did, how much resistance you used, and any other relevant information (injuries, unusual events that may have affected your workout, etc.). Use your log to accomplish these objectives:

- Adjust future workouts.
- Increase the intensity of your training session.
- Measure your improvement.
- Identify weaknesses in your training program.
- Help motivate you to continue exercising.

Muscles Do Matter

Raising your level of muscular fitness can have a corresponding effect on the quality of your life. Not only will you be able to better handle the demands of daily living, you'll feel better and be less likely to suffer the nagging injuries that seem all too prevalent among most people. As such, keep in mind that muscles do matter—for all people in all walks of life.

CHAPTER TEN

DEVELOPING FLEXIBILITY

Properly stretched muscles provide you with an enhanced capability for easy, pain-free movement.

Touching your toes. Reaching overhead to a shelf that is almost beyond your reach. Scratching the middle of your back. A few examples of the daily tasks in your life that involve flexibility, the functional capacity of the skeletal joints in your body to move through a normal range of motion. The flexibility level of each of your body's skeletal joints is related to the relative "tightness" of the various soft tissues that affect the ability of each specific joint to move (joint capsule, muscles, tendons, and ligaments). Of the four types of tissues, the one that tends to have the greatest impact on your level of flexibility and the one over which you have the most flexibility control is your musculature. It follows that since a greater level of elasticity in the muscles surrounding a joint enables that joint to more easily move through its full range of motion (ROM), exercises that stretch your muscles will increase your level of flexibility.

Why Stretch?

Simply stated, stretching is good for you. Your muscles are designed to be long, flexible, and lean. When they're in that condition, they provide you with an enhanced capability for easy, pain-free movement.

Stretching can also help you deal with emotional pressures. For example, when you're under stress, your muscles tend to contract involuntarily, thereby creating even more tension. Stretching helps your muscles to relax. As your muscles relax, so do you. Even though the factor(s) that contributed to your stress may still be present, proper stretching can be an excellent tension remedy.

A higher level of flexibility has also been shown to have a positive effect on your ability to perform almost all physical tasks—from relatively non-stressful activities such as sitting and walking to more vigorous activities such as jogging and playing sports. An increased level of flexibility can also make you "look better" by improving your posture and the way you carry yourself.

Finally (and perhaps most importantly), stretching is thought to help reduce the likelihood that you will be injured. By increasing your level of circulation and raising the temperature of your muscles, stretching before you exercise can help prepare your body for physical activities of all kinds. As a result, you will be much less likely to suffer muscle pulls and strains.

When Should You Stretch?

The times when stretching is most necessary are before and after working out. Because most physical activity (particularly sports) tend to involve less than full range-of-motion movements, most experts strongly recommend that you should also stretch after you exercise, as well as before. Accordingly, stretching properly should be an integral part of the warm-up and cool-down phases of your exercise regiment. Furthermore, all factors considered, a strong case can be made that you should stretch daily. You'll feel better and will be better prepared to handle the demands of your daily life. Fortunately, stretching can be performed at any opportune moment (e.g., when you first wake up in the morning, when you're driving, when you're watching television, when you're sitting at your desk, just before you go to bed, etc.).

How Should You Stretch?

In most critical tasks in life, one of the fundamental keys to being successful is to develop and implement an effective "action plan." Stretching is no different. An appropriate prescription for proper stretching involves a basic strategy that can mean the difference between you receiving all of the benefits of stretching or your harming yourself. Table 10-1 presents a basic stretching strategy that should be universally adopted. It's simple. It's easy to follow. It's based on sound science.

S tretch daily.

T ake your time. Stretch slowly.

R epeat each exercise four to six times before doing the next exercise.

E asy does it. Relax as you stretch.

T ry not to bounce. Avoid fast, jerky movements.

C oncentrate on breathing normally while you stretch.

H old each position for at least 10-30 seconds.

- Stretch daily. When it comes to stretching your muscles, gravity can be stiff competition. What you attempt to make more flexible, gravity works to contract and tighten. Accordingly, all factors considered, if you fail to stretch on a daily basis, the likelihood is that gravity will prevail. Your long, lean muscles will shorten and be more prone to injury.

- Take your time. Stretch slowly. Excessive force can be generated whenever you stretch too quickly. As you stretch, the momentum caused by your actions helps to take your muscles through their full range of motion. Slow, controlled momentum can increase your flexibility level without exposing you to a high risk of injury. Sharp, uncontrolled momentum, on the other hand, can jerk your muscles beyond their capacity and injure them. In this regard, the key is to control your movements—don't let them control you.

- Repeat each exercise four to six times before doing the next exercise. A wide variation of opinion exists about how many times you should do a particular exercise in your stretching regimen. As a rule, 4-6 repetitions will be sufficient. The exact number of repetitions, however, is an individual choice. You have to decide what is best for you. If you're a competitive or recreational athlete, for example, you may want to spend more time stretching (i.e., do more repetitions) than someone who engages in a more limited level of physical activity. One of the general guidelines you should follow when performing multiple repetitions of a given stretching exercise is to attempt to stretch a little bit further each time once you feel that you can comfortably perform that particular stretch.

- Easy does it. Relax as you stretch. When you're tense, your muscles tend to be tense. All other factors considered, tight muscles are relatively difficult to stretch. Relaxed muscles, on the other hand, can be more easily extended to their full range of motion. Accordingly, you should attempt to relax before and while you stretch.

- Try not to bounce. Avoid fast, jerky movements. Similar to stretching too quickly, bouncing while stretching results in uncontrolled momentum. Such momentum can pull your muscles sharply, forcing them to strain beyond their normal range of motion. As a result, whenever you bounce when you stretch, you risk the chance of causing microtears in your muscle fibers.

- Concentrate on breathing normally while you stretch. When you breathe normally, your breathing is relaxed. All factors considered, the more you're relaxed, the more relaxed are your muscles. Some individuals mistakenly believe that they should hold their breath while they're holding a stretch (i.e., at the mid-point of a stretching exercise). Keep in mind that if you hold your breath, you may deprive your muscles of the oxygen they need to function properly. Deprived of oxygen, your muscles may cramp.

- Hold each position for at least 10-30 seconds. Similar to the differences of opinion regarding how many repetitions of a particular stretching exercise you should do, no universally accepted guideline exists concerning how long you should hold a stretch. In this regard, the primary point to remember is that stretching involves "re-educating" your muscles. As you stretch, your muscles are "learning" new extensions of their range-of-motion capabilities. Within each muscle fiber is a structure referred to as a spindle. Spindles hold your muscle fibers in the position in which you stretch them. Accordingly, since the primary objective of stretching is to extend the range of motion of your muscles, you need to allow your muscles the opportunity to "learn" their new extension and then to maintain that position on their spindles. Because learning takes time, you need to give your muscles at least 10-30 seconds per repetition to "re-educate" themselves.

Recommended Stretching Guidelines

Besides the aforementioned basic stretching strategy, there are a number of additional points to consider when planning and executing your stretching program. Adherence to these factors will enhance both the effectiveness and the safety level of your stretching efforts. Among the stretching guidelines to which you should adhere are the following:

- Don't continue to stretch if you feel a sharp pain associated with the stretch or uncontrolled muscle cramping while stretching.

- Avoid vigorously stretching any area of your body that has been recently immobilized (i.e., placed in a cast).

- Don't overstretch a joint (i.e., stretch a joint only through its normal ROM).

- Don't stretch areas of your body that you previously have fractured until at least 8-12 weeks have passed since the fracture occurred. At that time, gentle stretching may be initiated.

- If you have or suspect you have osteoporosis, be particularly cautious while stretching.

- Be sensitive to the fact that if any mild soreness associated with your stretching efforts lasts longer than 24 hours, you probably exerted excessive force while stretching.

- Combine strengthening and stretching exercises so that any gains you achieve in joint mobility are accomplished concurrently with gains in the strength and stability of the given joints.

Recommended Fundamental Stretching Exercises

You have a wide variety of exercises to choose from when planning and organizing your stretching program. The 16 exercises in Figure 10-1 have been excerpted with permission from the 20th edition of *Stretching* by Bob Anderson, illustrations by Jean Anderson, published by Shelter Publications. While your selection of stretches is essentially an individual matter, you need to include exercises for each of the five major areas of your body (back; legs and hips; trunk; shoulders and arms; and head and neck). In addition, if you suffer from lower back pain, you should (whenever possible) perform stretching exercises from a seated or prone position, as opposed to a standing position, because such actions will lessen the strain on your back.

Taking Care of Your Body

A strong argument can be made that stretching on a regular basis is an essential step in taking care of your body. Over time, every day that you neglect to stretch, your body will suffer the negative consequences. To rework an old cliché, "A stretch a day can help keep you feeling OK". Simplistic, maybe. True, absolutely.

Before and After
Aerobic Exercise

Do a mild warm-up of 2–3 minutes before stretching.

Figure 10-1a

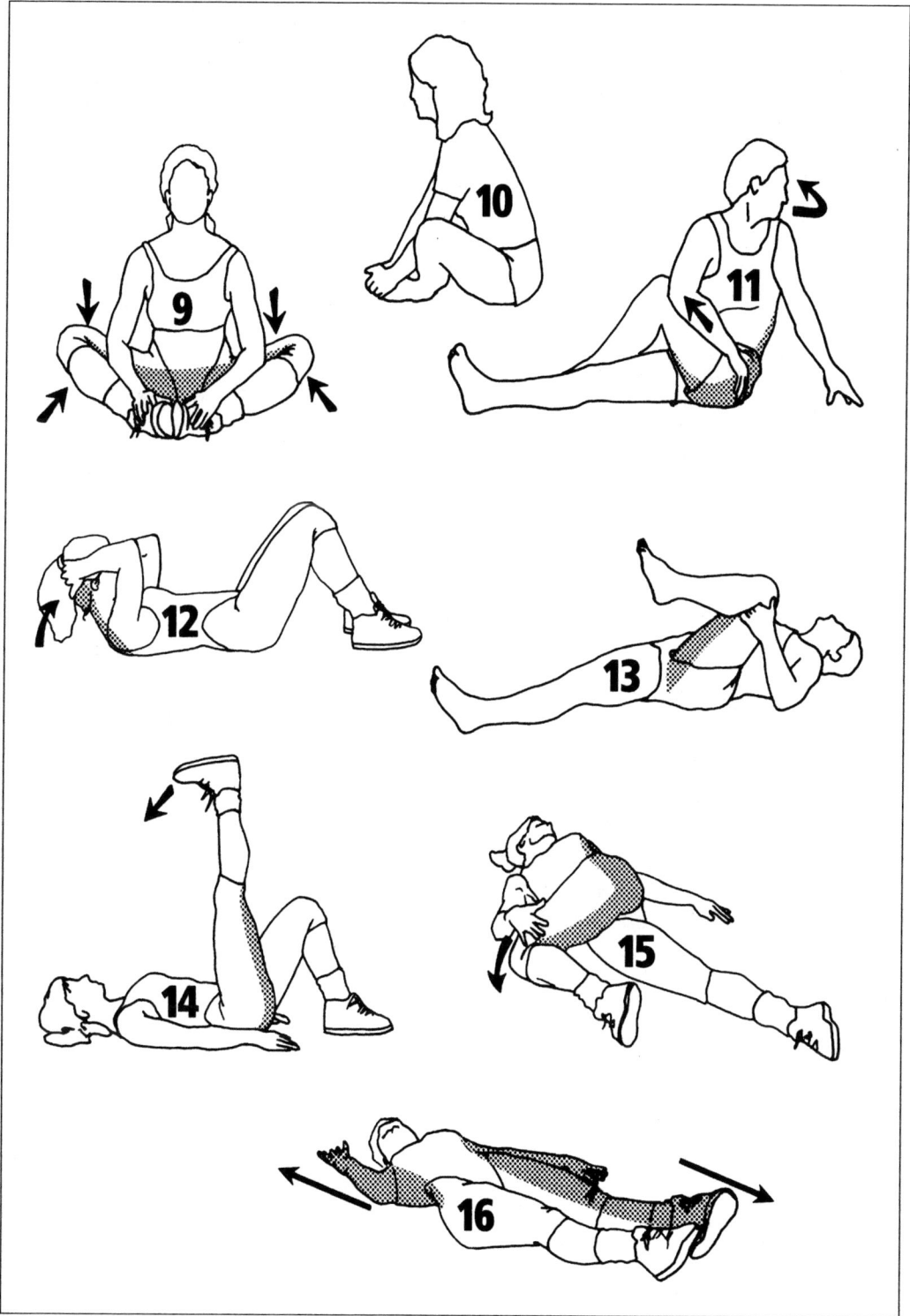

Figure 10-1b

Simply stated, stretching is good for you.

CHAPTER ELEVEN

LOSING WEIGHT SENSIBLY

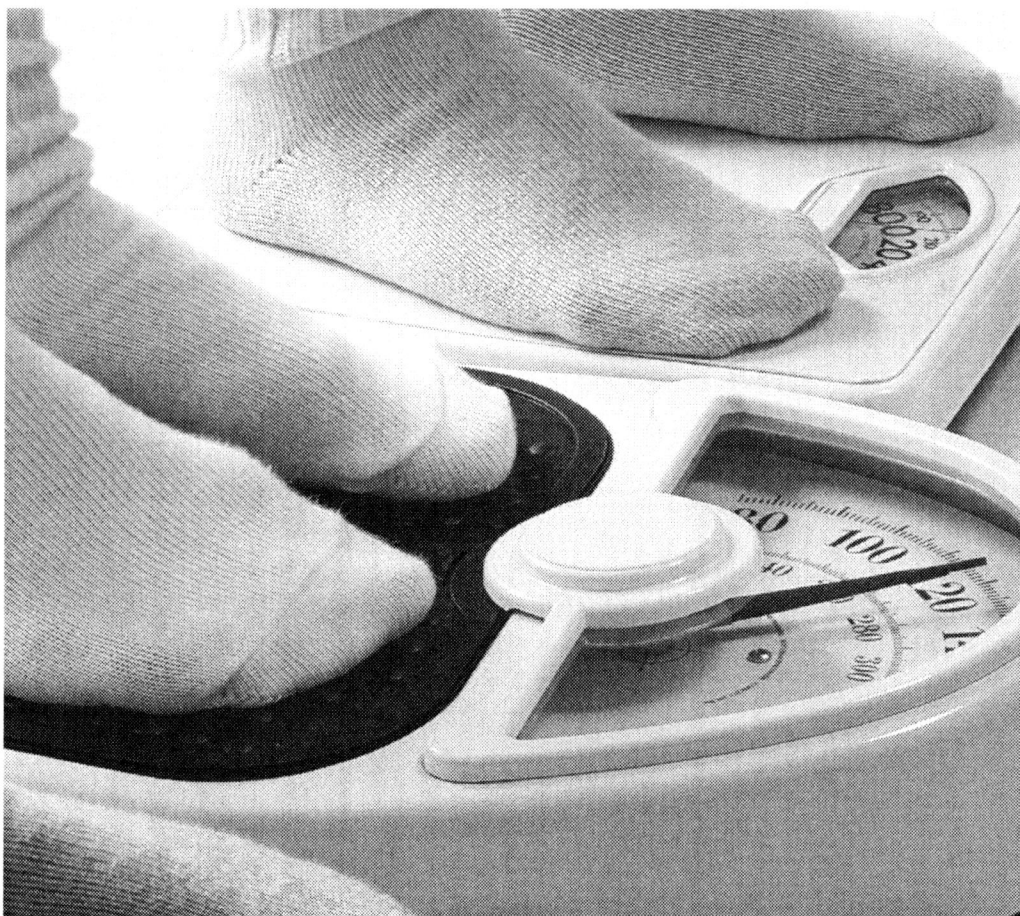

You should strive for achieving a body weight that is compatible
with a healthy lifestyle.

The challenge of maintaining a healthy weight is something many Americans face. In this country, for example, approximately 50 million men and 60 million women ages 18 to 79 are overweight. In an attempt to reverse this statistic, over 20 million adults are dieting to lose weight, while another 20 million think they should be dieting. In their quest to win the losing game, Americans are spending more than 40 billion dollars a year on the latest diet books, products, and services.

Concurrently, a number of people are also suffering from eating disorders such as anorexia nervosa and bulimia. Unfortunately, too many individuals who are looking to lose weight are also looking for a "quick fix." They want a way to lose weight fast with as little effort as possible. This quick-fix mentality has spawned a number of fad diets and practices such as the starvation diet, fasting, the grapefruit diet, the high-protein/low-carbohydrate diet, the high-fat/low-carbohydrate diet, pills and expensive potions etc.

Millions of Americans have attempted to follow these types of diets and practices in the hope that they have finally found something that might actually work for them. Unfortunately, what they don't know is that they may be doing themselves more harm than good. Eventually, most of these individuals reach the inevitable conclusion that what they're doing simply doesn't work. So if the vast array of popular diets and weight-loss practices don't work, what can you do to lose weight and to keep the weight off? Before attempting to answer that question, however, you need to address the issue of "how much should you actually weigh."

How Much Should You Weigh?

The perceptions of many individuals about what constitutes an appropriate or ideal body weight tend to be somewhat distorted or misguided. As such, countless Americans are frustrated by their inability (due to a perceived lack of willpower) to lose those final few pounds. These individuals become obsessed with reaching some "mythical" ideal body weight. Their obsession is frequently manifested in a very counterproductive manner. Initially at least, these individuals view "food" as their archenemy—something to be ingested only when their willpower could not sustain them any longer. Many of them also exercise incessantly. Regrettably, most of these suffer a relapse in their commitment to eat less and exercise more, causing them to feel like an incorrigible failure. Are these individuals really failures, or are they the victims of unrealistic goals and expectations?

The Concept of Ideal Body Weight

Perhaps the most commonly used method for assessing whether you are within your ideal body weight range is a height-weight table. Unfortunately, a number of problems exist with using height-weight tables to determine your ideal body weight. For example, the body weights in these tables are considered to be desirable only on the basis that they had a positive correlation with longevity for the population studied—they do not take into account the health problems that are frequently associated with obesity.

The members of the first group ever studied for this purpose were subscribers to Metropolitan Life Insurance. Obviously, however, this particular group of individuals is not representative of the general population (in fact, few minorities or individuals of lower socioeconomic status were included). Furthermore, the body weights of these individuals were only measured once (if at all—since many individuals verbally reported their body weights and were never actually weighed). The information regarding the applicants' body weights was only obtained at the time that the individuals initially applied for the life insurance. No information was obtained regarding changes in body weight or the development of health problems after the insurance policies were initially purchased. These problems aside, the fundamental weakness of height-weight tables is that they do not assess body composition (i.e., the relative amount of body fat that comprises your total body weight).

Because the relative percentage of body fat of your body has more important implications concerning your health and functional capabilities than does your total body weight, some believe that a specific ideal body weight can be established once your percent body fat is known. Such a conclusion is a somewhat shortsighted view for a number of reasons. Since all of the available techniques for measuring body composition only provide an estimate of percent body fat, the resulting calculations are subject to error. For example, hydrostatic (underwater) weighing, the accepted "gold standard" for analyzing body composition, has a statistically acceptable margin of error of approximately plus or minus two to three percent. The more commonly employed techniques such as skinfold measurements and bioelectrical impedance have margins of error that are even higher (i.e., approximately plus or minus five percent).

Unfortunately, even if your percent body fat could be accurately and precisely assessed, additional information would be needed to determine your ideal body weight. How much body fat you have may not matter as much as where it is located on your body.

Considerable evidence indicates that the location of fat deposits on your body determines how easy it is for you to lose weight, and increases your risk of developing a number of health-related problems. The location of the fat that is deposited on your body is classified into two basic categories: male-pattern (graphically depicted as apple-shaped) and female-pattern (graphically depicted as pear-shaped). Despite their illustrative names, each type of fat pattern can occur in both sexes, although men usually tend to be "apples" and women typically are classified as "pears." "Apples" characteristically deposit high amounts of fat in the abdominal and trunk regions, while "pears" deposit high amounts of fat in the hip, buttocks, and thigh regions.

The waist-to-hip ratio (WHR) is a simple, yet accurate, method for determining your personal distribution pattern for body fat. Your waist-to-hip ratio is determined by dividing your waist circumference by your hip circumference. Waist circumference is defined as the smallest circumference between your rib cage and belly button. Hip circumference is defined as the largest circumference of your hip-buttocks region. Men with WHR values exceeding 1.00 are considered "apples," while women with WHR values above 0.80 are considered "apples."

Available evidence suggests that individuals with fat distributed on their upper body (apples) are highly prone to "the deadly quartet" of risk factors for coronary heart disease—high blood pressure, type II (non-insulin dependent) diabetes, elevated levels of triglycerides (hypertriglyceridemia), and low levels of high density lipoproteins ("good cholesterol") in their blood. The greater your exposure to these four factors, the higher your risk of heart disease. All news is not bad for "apples," however. Weight loss (particularly fat loss) tends to be easier for "apples," because they benefit from the high turnover rate of abdominal adipocytes (fat cells). Unfortunately, for individuals classified as "pears," weight loss is more difficult because the fat cells that are located in their hip, buttock, and thigh regions do not easily relinquish their fat—a fact to which many "pears" who have attempted to lose weight can readily attest.

Ideal for What?

To determine your ideal body weight, you shouldn't rely solely on a bathroom scale, height-weight tables, or percent body fat measurements. What represents a safe, realistic, and perhaps more importantly attainable body weight for you will depend (to a large extent) on the following factors:

- Medical history. Your current medical history, to include a thoughtful review of your personal health risk factors should be taken into account when attempting to define your ideal body weight. For example, if your blood pressure is elevated, a modest weight reduction could be quite beneficial. Extra body mass means that your heart must work harder to pump blood through miles of extra capillaries that feed that extra tissue. Type II diabetes and blood lipid-lipoprotein profiles are further examples of medical conditions that can be positively affected by weight loss.

- Family history. Body weight, like most other physical characteristics, is strongly influenced by genetic factors. If your parents and siblings are extremely overweight, it is highly unlikely that you will ever be "model-thin." As unfair as such a judgement might at first appear, such a limitation should be kept in mind when establishing your ideal body-weight goals.

- Body fat distribution. As previously stated, body fat located in your upper body region is very risky in terms of your health. If you possess a high amount of upper body fat (as determined by your WHR), you should consider losing weight (specifically body fat) through a combined program of sensible eating and exercise.

- Functional ability. If your existing body weight inhibits your ability to either effectively and efficiently perform your activities of daily living or comfortably engage in the recreational pursuits of your choice, it is probably not at an ideal level.

Losing Weight

The answer to sensible weight loss is actually relatively simple: you must commit to a lifelong habit of sensible eating, sensible behavior, and regular exercise.

In other words, losing weight should be an integral part of your plan for total fitness. As such, the essential elements of your strategy to lose weight and keep it off should be diet, exercise, and behavioral modification (to facilitate your efforts to eat sensibly). Keep in mind that weight loss isn't something that can or should happen fast. It is essentially a slow process that requires discipline, education, planning, and setting realistic goals. How much you eat, what you eat, and how much you exercise are factors that you generally can control. Provided that you are reasonably motivated to lose weight, it should be relatively easy to get on the right track. Some factors exist, however, over which you have little or no control. You need to learn to deal with these factors appropriately.

One of these factors is your genetics. The genes you were born with can affect whether you have a "weight problem." There is no way around this. If both of your parents were overweight, there is a good chance of you being overweight also. Accordingly, if you are genetically predisposed to weight gain, eating right and exercising regularly should definitely be a top priority for you. Two other factors over which you have no control, and both of which have a bearing on body weight, are age and race.

How much you eat and your ability to lose weight may also be affected by certain psychological factors. These factors include all of the non-biological reasons that people eat. Keep in mind that the feeling of being hungry is not always the reason for eating. Your emotions have a big effect on what and when you eat. Any emotion such as stress, boredom, loneliness, anxiety, depression and fatigue increase the likelihood of overeating. Also, you may simply eat out of habit i.e. time to eat, being in the presence of those who are eating and exposure to sight and smell of food. During breaks at work or when watching television at night, some individuals routinely head for the lunch pail, cupboard, or refrigerator. These behavioral patterns can be very hard to break. In such cases, you need to plan ahead carefully. Keep healthy foods readily available, limit the quantity and availability of high fat and high sugar foods and self monitor food taken and exercise.

Another factor to keep in mind with regard to weight loss is that whatever efforts you may have undertaken to substantially limit your caloric intake in the past may hinder chances of losing weight in the future. The more times that you have restricted your caloric intake previously, the harder it will be to lose weight the next time. When calories are not coming into your body on a regular basis, your body thinks it is starving and must hang on to every calorie that is consumed. In response, your body automatically slows down the rate at which it burns calories for energy (i.e., its metabolic rate) to conserve every available calorie.

Your metabolic rate has a huge effect on how many calories your body uses to function. Your resting metabolic rate represents the energy your body expends to maintain life and normal bodily operations, such as breathing, brain function and digestion. About 60-75% of the calories you expend on a daily basis support these operations. When you limit your intake of calories, your resting metabolic rate eventually decreases because your body is trying to conserve energy. Because your body has to have fuel to maintain life and to perform certain essential bodily functions, any number of consumed calories, no matter how small, are saved for these purposes. If your body receives a steady and adequate number of calories, it will recognize the fact that it doesn't have to worry about conserving fuel. In the process, your body continues to function as it normally does. Accordingly, to prevent your metabolism from slowing down, your calorie intake should never fall below 1000-1200 calories per day.

The more lean muscle mass you have and the more your muscles are used while exercising, the more calories you will burn, and the higher your metabolic rate will remain. Muscle tissue is more metabolically active than fat tissue. One pound of muscle tissue burns about 40 calories a day just to maintain itself; one pound of fat, on the other hand, burns only about two calories a day. To a limited extent, you can change the amount of muscle that you have by strength training.

Exercising on a Regular Basis

Because the two most important factors in keeping your weight at a desirable level are sensible eating and regular exercise, you can take great strides to win the losing game by exercising on a regular basis. The U.S. Surgeon General reports that to be healthy, individuals should get about 30 minutes of moderate exercise on most, if not all, days of the week. In reality, most Americans do not for a period of time even close to this amount. Statistics that show that a sedentary lifestyle is the leading cause of obesity in the United States help confirm the need to be physically active. In fact, too many people who have relatively sedentary desk jobs usually sit in front of a television set or at a computer when they come home from work at night. As a result, they burn fewer calories and store more fat than do more physically active people.

Exercise can have a positive impact on your weight control efforts in a number of ways. For example, if you exercise on a regular basis, your body will burn calories faster.

Also, strength training can help build muscle tissue, which will help keep your resting metabolic rate at a higher level. Exercise will also help you look better, even if you don't lose a lot of weight. Because muscle is more dense and heavy than fat, replacing fat with muscle will cause you to look more fit and trim. Your waistline will be smaller even if your total body weight remains unchanged.

Exercise should definitely be something you find enjoyable or you are not going to want to do it. While any physical activity that you enjoy should promote some measure of weight loss, the most effective exercise program for losing weight should include both aerobic conditioning and strength training. Aerobic conditioning not only burns calories and fat, it is also the best type of exercise for strengthening your heart muscle. Strength training, on the other hand, doesn't use many calories. More importantly, however, it enables you to maintain (and in some instances to increase) your level of lean muscle mass. As was stated previously, the higher your level of lean muscle mass, the higher your metabolic rate, since muscle is the most metabolically active tissue in your body.

When selecting aerobic exercises that will maximize your efforts to lose weight, you should choose those that involve the largest muscle groups in your body, such as your legs and buttocks. Aerobic exercise should be rhythmic, should raise your heart rate and should slightly increase your rate of breathing. Some examples of aerobic activities that are particularly appropriate for losing weight are walking, hiking, running, cycling, rowing, mechanical stair climbing, swimming and aerobic dance. Many sporting and athletic activities meet the criteria for aerobic exercise.

Considerable disagreement exists concerning which approach to aerobic exercise is better for weight loss: high-intensity for a short duration or low-intensity for a long duration. A common misconception is that low-intensity exercise is the best way to train if you want to lose weight since a higher percentage of fat calories is being burned for fuel than is the case with high- intensity exercise. In fact, your body doesn't need to be very efficient during low-intensity exercise. As a result, your body can take more time to free up fatty acids and burn those as fuel. During high-intensity exercise, however, your body must create energy very quickly, no matter what the source. Accordingly, your body uses stored carbohydrates, rather than stored fat, as an energy source because carbohydrates are easier to utilize. Because your body will replace fat calories lost more quickly than carbohydrate calories, you have a much better chance of keeping any weight you lose off longer if your weight loss primarily involves expended carbohydrates.

Exercising at a low level of intensity offers two noteworthy benefits with regard to weight loss. First, because it is easier to perform, you are more likely to stick with your exercise program. Second, because it tends to place fewer orthopedic stresses on the joints of your body, it is safer and involves less physical discomfort. Both factors are especially important for individuals who are very unfit, obese, or who are just starting an exercise program.

When you're attempting to lose weight, the main point to keep in mind is that it is the total number of calories you expend while exercising, not what percentage of those calories comes from either fat or carbohydrates. Although you may expend a higher percentage of fat calories at a lower level of exercise intensity, you will burn a higher number of fat calories if you exercise at a higher intensity. The bottom line is that the harder you exercise, the more calories you burn (and the more weight you lose).

Although it does not involve the expenditure of very many calories, strength training is another type of exercise that can greatly enhance your weight-loss efforts. Strength training can help you build and maintain your level of lean muscle, the tissue in your body that burns the most calories because it is very metabolically active. All factors considered, the more lean muscle mass you have, the easier it is for you to win the losing game.

Adopting a Sensible Eating Plan

Possibly the most difficult step to master in your efforts to lose weight and keep it off is to adopt a sensible eating plan. You should keep in mind that even small changes in your diet can make a big impact on your weight-loss efforts. A sensible diet for losing weight should be relatively low in calories but should never fall below about 10-12 calories per pound of your current body weight. Your body needs this many calories to perform its necessary bodily functions and to maintain life. A sound diet should provide all the nutrients you need to be healthy. It should include foods that you like, as long as they are nutritious. When deciding what to eat on your diet, you should also consider the expense, availability, and ease of preparation of the various foodstuffs. Finally, you should adopt an eating plan that you likely will be able to stick with for an extended period of time.

The first step in developing a sensible eating plan is to determine what your caloric needs are so that you consume an adequate number of calories, but not so many that you can not lose weight. The simplest way to calculate an appropriate daily caloric intake is for you to multiply your current weight (in pounds) by 15 calories. Twelve of these calories help meet your minimum basal metabolic needs, while three of these calories can satisfy your energy expenditures during physical activity. For example, if you are a 150-pound person, you need 2250 calories daily to sustain your body weight.

The next step is to reduce your calculated daily caloric total by 250 calories. By subtracting 250 calories from your normal diet and burning an additional 250 calories a day by exercising, you can reasonably expect to lose one pound a week. Because one pound of body fat contains 3500 calories, a deficit of 500 calories per day should result in a loss of one pound a week (seven days a week x 500 fewer calories = 3500 fewer calories = one lost pound of fat). While losing one pound of fat per week may seem to be an incredibly slow pace, this approach is actually the safest way for your body to achieve permanent weight loss. A relatively slow weight loss is much more likely to be sustained than the "quick fix" approach because your body will be less likely to disturb (i.e., lower) your resting metabolic rate.

Decreasing 250 calories a day from your diet might seem like a lot, but actually relatively simple ways exist to help make a reduction like this on a daily basis. For example, when eating a meal at home or in a restaurant, limit yourself to just one portion. At home, take your one portion and wrap up the leftovers right away to discourage nibbling. Restaurant portions tend to be very large, so try eating just half of the entree and have the other half wrapped up to take home for the next day. When eating at home, try eating your meals on small plates. This way, it will not look like you're depriving yourself. Also, chew your food slowly. Take smaller bites and enjoy every one. It takes the brain about 20 minutes to realize that your stomach is full. In this amount of time, most people tend to eat everything on their plates.

Another way to sensibly eat less is to forget about cleaning your plate. Rather than eating everything, stop when you're full. Also, when enjoying a meal, try to make that the only activity on which you're focusing. For example, watching television or reading while eating can be distractions. By sitting down and concentrating on your food, you are more likely to enjoy the meal, and you won't be as likely to eat past the point of feeling full. If a craving for high-fat foods is a problem, try to keep such foods out of your residence entirely. If the rest of your family wants to eat cake and ice cream, try to keep those items and similar snacks in an out-of-the-way cupboard or deep in the freezing compartment of your refrigerator (i.e., out of sight, out of mind).

Eating less, but more frequently, can also facilitate your weight-loss efforts. This approach can help keep your blood sugar levels steady and discourage the onset of hunger pangs that might lead you to snack. Some evidence suggests that adequate calcium in the diet and adequate protein can help keep blood sugar levels stable and support continual weight loss.

Skipping meals or eating only once or twice a day can hinder your efforts to lose weight. Your body likes to have a steady source of fuel throughout the day. That way your body never has to fear that it is in starvation mode, and it can keep functioning normally without "hanging on" to every calorie. The best way to ensure that your body has a steady source of fuel is to eat three regular meals a day, or five or six smaller meals daily.

For example, choose a diet that has plenty of fruits, vegetables, and grain products. Also, try to keep your diet low in fat, saturated fat, and cholesterol. Sugar, salt, and alcoholic beverages should be consumed in moderation. Your diet should also contain adequate amounts of carbohydrates, protein and fat. Carbohydrates are your body's preferred source of fuel and should make up the bulk of your diet.

Foods high in complex carbohydrates, as well as fruits and vegetables, are also sources of fiber. Fiber is very important in your diet because it fills you up and allows you to feel satisfied, while adding very few calories to your diet. Fiber also aids in moving food, nutrients and toxins quickly through your digestive tract. This feature lowers your risk of developing colon cancer because those toxins are not sitting around in your digestive tract. Rather they are being cleaned out regularly. You should aim at consuming 25-40 grams of fiber a day. The best sources of fiber are fruits and vegetables, whole grains, legumes, seeds, and oats.

Finally, you should drink substantial amounts of water daily. Your body begins experiencing dehydration before you even know you're thirsty. When the systems of your body do not have enough water, your body's cells, (which use water for every function they perform), will start extracting water from your bloodstream. When your blood is cycled back through your heart, your heart realizes that there is not enough water and triggers the thirst response that you typically experience. Once you start replacing water in your system, it is a bit late. Your body has been dehydrated and has a lot of work to do to compensate for that condition. To prevent this, you should drink water often, even when you don't feel thirsty. As a rule, about 8-10 glasses of water a day should be sufficient. On days when you exercise or on very hot days, you may need even more water to replace what you have lost through perspiration.

A Recipe for Success

It is quite evident that everyone cannot, and should not, be as thin as the proverbial "Hollywood" or "Madison Avenue" ideal body type. Common sense and sound nutrition principles mandate that you should avoid setting "hard and fast" body-weight goals for yourself. Rather, you should strive for achieving a body weight that is compatible with a healthy lifestyle. All factors considered, the body weight that results from adopting such a lifestyle should ultimately be considered as the ideal union between your wellness level, your genetic potential, and reality. In this regard, eating sensibly and exercising regularly is a sound recipe for losing weight and keeping it off.

CHAPTER TWELVE

CHOOSING THE

'RIGHT' EXERCISE

If you select a way to exercise that is compatible with your needs and interests, you heighten the likelihood that you will stick with your exercise program.

How should you exercise? Run? Swim? Aerobic Dance Working out on a machine such as a treadmill, exercise cycle, or a cross trainer -   does it really matter? It does. In fact, deciding which type of exercise you want to engage in can be one of the most important decisions you can make concerning your exercise program.

Thoughtfully reached, such a decision can enhance the likelihood that you can achieve your exercise-related goals and objectives. Carelessly reached, such an approach to the issue can have negative consequences for you as an exerciser. For example, if you select a way to exercise that is incompatible with your needs and interests, you heighten the likelihood of diminishing your level of exercise compliance, reducing the level of results that you gain from your exercise regimen, creating an unbridgeable conflict between their expectations and the results you achieve by exercising, and increasing your risk of sustaining an injury while exercising.

Unfortunately, some individuals don't purposefully consider their exercise options. Rather, they either address the matter in a relatively hasty manner or use a subjective "feeling" or "gut reaction" to make their choice of what modality to employ when exercising. As a result, they may compromise their exercise efforts.

Making a Suitable Choice

Once you decide that it is in your best interests to engage in the type of exercise that offers you the best relative choice, (all factors considered) you should then attempt to determine which exercise activity is, in fact, the "right" one for you. In essence, you should address the task as you would any other important personal decision in your life.

For example, the process of selecting which exercise tool to use should embody the fundamental steps normally inherent in a sound decision-making process—set a goal (i.e., ascertain the "right" exercise modality); identify possible solutions for achieving your specified goal (i.e., stair climbing machine, roller blading, strength training, rowing, stationary exercise bike, jogging, swimming, etc.); establish criteria for evaluating each possible solution (i.e., safety, cost, etc.); apply the criteria to each alternative course of action; and make the appropriate decision (choice).

Of the various steps involved in the normal decision-making process, perhaps the most problematic is deciding which criteria you should use to assess the relative merits of your various modality options. In this regard, the acronym "S.S.A.F.F.E.E.E." can provide you with meaningful guidelines for making such a decision. While assigning a priority weighting to each of the eight possible criteria is essentially a subjective (i.e., personal) matter, using "S.S.A.F.F.E.E.E." can help you make a relative judgment concerning the "good" and "bad" aspects of each of your respective choices.

S.S.A.F.F.E.E.E. CRITERIA

A brief overview of the eight criteria in the "S.S.A.F.F.E.E.E." acronym includes the following points:

- <u>S</u> cientifically documented benefits. All stated claims and counterclaims concerning a specific exercise modality should be scientifically corroborated. In this regard, such research should be independently (i.e., by an unbiased, outside research team) conducted on a double-blind basis with an appropriate study design and control groups. Preferably, the results of this research would be published in a refereed professional journal. In other words, your chosen mode of exercising should offer confirmed benefits (unlike many of the so called exercise devices promoted on television—e.g., magnets, thigh machines, etc.).

- <u>S</u> afe. An exercise modality should not subject you to excessive force or stress on any part or joint of your body. While no exercise activity can ever be considered 100% safe, some activities are obviously safer than others. For example, walking and machine-based stair climbing place lower orthopedic stress on your lower body than running.

- <u>A</u> ppropriate to your unique needs and situation. Every potential exercise enthusiast tends to have qualities, characteristics, and idiosyncrasies that can affect the degree to which a particular exercise modality is appropriate for that person. For example, the cost of engaging in a specific modality may preclude you from using a particular exercise mode if you have limited financial resources. Convenience, lifestyle, and existing fitness level are examples of other factors that you should consider concerning their impact on whether a specific exercise modality is appropriate for you.

- <u>F</u> unctionally sound. All factors considered, the more functional the exercise experience, the more applicable and beneficial the consequences of that exercise bout to "real-life" activities. In recent years, the functionality of a given activity has been addressed by proponents of a movement theory that is popularly referred to as "closed chain exercise." It is much more beneficial, they claim, for you to train in a "natural" manner that involves weight-bearing, multi-joint exercise. The less desirable (and less functional) way to exercise is to engage in non-weight-bearing activity—one that frequently stresses muscles or muscle groups in an isolated (i.e., "unnatural") manner.

- <u>F</u> eel. Depending on how they are engineered, exercise machines have a mechanical level of efficiency that affects the experiential "feel" of the machine. All factors considered, the larger the range of this level of efficiency, the greater the likelihood that you will be able to match your personal level of mechanical efficiency with the exercise modality you are using. In sports, this level of efficiency is sometimes referred to as an athlete's "wheel house" (i.e., a stroked tennis ball looks larger than normal when it is coming at you). In the exercise arena, this aspect is often perceived to affect the degree to which you can get into your personal "comfort zone."

- E ffective. Like everyone else, your exercise efforts are geared to achieve specific results. All factors being equal, the higher the level of particular results you can gain from a specific type of exercise activity, the more desirable the modality. Furthermore, the results you achieve by exercising are typically the most important single factor in whether you stick with your exercise regimen.

- E njoyment. Exercise can and should be fun. A beneficial exercise experience should not be drudgery and should not be painful. If it is, the likelihood of you sticking with your exercise regimen is greatly diminished. Accordingly, you should always select an activity that you enjoy for your exercise modality of choice.

MAKING THE "RIGHT" CHOICE

Once you decide to exercise, you usually have a number or options to choose from regarding which exercise modality to use. Nonetheless, your choice should not be made in a haphazard manner. Rather, the actual modality selected should be the result of a thoughtful, well-considered process. While several modalities may meet most (if not all) of the suggested evaluative criteria, you have a personal responsibility to decide which modality is most "right" for you. Anything less might compromise your exercise efforts. As an extrapolation of the traditional axiom might dictate, it is much better for you to be "S.S.A.F.F.E.E." than sorry.

CHAPTER THIRTEEN

EXERCISE AND

WOMEN'S ISSUES

Exercise can and should be an integral part of every woman's lifestyle.

In recent years, more and more women of all ages are taking advantage of the numerous benefits of exercise. As these women train and push their bodies to their ever-expanding limits, several important issues that may impact on a woman's exercise efforts need to be considered including the physiological differences between men and women, the female triad, osteoporosis, eating disorders, menopause, premenstrual syndrome, musculoskeletal concerns, breast protection while exercising, pre- and postnatal physical activity. Addressing these factors can help women design and engage in a more medically sound exercise program.

Physiological Differences between Men and Women

Men and women are different physically. Quite different. In fact, more than 150 physiological differences between men and women have been identified. To a point, these differences affect how a woman should exercise and the degree to which she will realize a specifically desired training effect.

Women, on the average, are more flexible, more coordinated, less tolerant of excessive heat, and have a greater level of balance. Men, on the other hand, tend to be stronger, faster, and more powerful. A list of the gender-based differences that could possibly have an impact on a woman's exercise efforts includes the following:

- A woman's lower center of gravity (6% lower than that of a male) enhances her ability to perform activities that involve balance and hinders her capacity to do exercise that involves rotary movement (i.e., she can't run as fast).

- The tendency to accumulate fat on her waist, arms, and thighs (as opposed to where men deposit fat—on their back, chest, and abdomen) diminishes a woman's movement efficiency.

- Women have a higher heart rate (5-8 bpm higher than men) both at rest and at all levels of exercise.

- The larger male heart and lungs force more blood from the heart on each beat (i.e., a higher stroke volume) and allow a greater volume of air to be expelled from the lungs following a maximal inspiration (i.e., vital capacity) than those of a woman.

- Women have less bone mass, less muscle component, but more fat than men. This combination of more fat and less muscle per unit volume has a negative effect upon a woman's ability to do activities requiring strength, speed, and power.

- Women are more flexible than men—a trait that enhances their capacity to engage in full-range movements (i.e., a skill that is utilized while reaching for a ball, throwing, kicking, etc.).

- Men have a higher percentage of red blood cells, the oxygen-carrying component in the body, and have a greater amount (30%) of total body hemoglobin due to their larger body size. As a result, during vigorous exercise, women have to increase their heart rate since stroke volume and performance are limited by total blood volume. Accordingly, for a given submaximal work load, women are always operating at a level closer to their maximum than men, and will reach exhaustion sooner.

- Men have a higher capacity to continue to consume and deliver the oxygen that is required by muscles that are exercising at various workloads.

- A woman has an angular displacement of her forearm to her upper arm (i.e., when she extends her arms straight in front of her with her palms up, her elbows tend to form an "x," whereas a man's arms form parallel lines when they're extended in a similar manner) that hinders her ability to throw and handicaps her in sporting activities that involve maximum leverage, such as tennis.

- Another physiological difference is the angle of the femur with the pelvis. A woman's pelvis is slightly (0.5 inch) wider and is rounder than a man's. From her slightly wider pelvis, a woman's femurs extend at a greater angle. It appears that the tendency of a woman's legs to form an x-shape when extended, her distended joints, and the softer joints and ligaments in her pelvic girdle collectively place a woman at a disadvantage in running and jumping activities.

- Because women possess only about half the amount of lean muscle mass than their male counterparts, they do not perform as well as men in activities that require explosive power (e.g., sprinting, jumping, etc.) Even when size is held constant, women are only about 80% as strong as men.

- Women have a higher body temperature at rest than men, fewer sweat glands, lower sweat production, and a propensity to start sweating at higher temperatures than do men. A woman's greater amount of adipose tissue serves as insulation and inhibits heat dissipation. These differences have an important implication for physical performance. Because women have less tolerance to heat than men, women are more subject to heat stress than men. Under heat conditions and at low levels of work, a woman's heart rate is 20-30 beats/min faster. Accordingly, under higher levels of heat condition, a woman has to work relatively harder than a man to achieve similar workloads.

The Female Triad

Some athletic women face a risk that they may develop one or more of three medical disorders, collectively known as the female triad. The female triad refers to the interrelatedness of three medical disorders: disordered eating, amenorrhea, and osteoporosis. These young women, driven to excel in their chosen activities and pressured to fit a specific body image (e.g., leanness, low percent body fat, or lower weight) in order to attain their sports-related performance goals, place themselves at risk for the development of disordered patterns of eating. Such eating behavior may lead to menstrual dysfunction and, subsequently, premature osteoporosis. By itself, each disorder can be a significant medical concern, but, collectively, the potential for far more serious health consequences and a higher risk of mortality exists.

Disordered Eating

Disordered eating refers to the array of abnormal patterns of eating that is characterized by the use of laxatives, diuretics, and diet pills, bingeing and/or vomiting, severe calorie restriction, food avoidance, and fasting. The two main types of eating disorders are anorexia nervosa (self-starvation) and bulimia nervosa (bingeing and purging).

Some of the diagnostic signs for anorexia nervosa are maintenance of low body weight (>85% of ideal body weight), intense fear of gaining weight, distorted body image, and absence of menstrual cycles for at leas three months (amenorrhea). Bulimia nervosa can be detected if any of the following signs are present: binge eating at least twice a week for three months, excessive behaviors to avoid weight gain, preoccupation with body shape and size, vomiting, use of laxatives and/or diuretics, and excessive exercise.

The incidence of eating disorders among female athletes greatly exceeds that of the general public. A number or factors can lead to disordered eating, including societal pressures to be thin, family culture, low self-esteem and depression, physical or sexual abuse, or pressure from coaches to be thin. Sport-specific pressures, such as subjective scoring based on appearance and weight categories for participation, can also contribute to eating disorders.

There are several serious consequences associated with disordered eating. The most common of these effects include abnormally low resting heart rate and blood pressure and other heart dysrhythmias, electrolyte disturbances, low red and white blood cell count, decreased ability of blood to clot, hormonal alterations, decline in immune function, gastrointestinal disease/digestive problems, decrease in endurance, strength and speed, and an increased risk of injury.

Amenorrhea

A woman's normal menstrual cycle is 21-36 days. Primary amenorrhea is a condition in which menstruation has not begun by age 16. Secondary amenorrhea is the absence of a menstrual cycle for three to six months and is most prevalent among female athletes. The most common type of amenorrhea is oligomenorrhea, which means infrequent menstrual cycles.

Several factors can contribute to amenorrhea, such as the physical stress of exercise, low body weight, low body fat, physiological stress, energy drain, poor diet, pregnancy, early menopause and certain types of tumors. Amenorrhea typically affects long-distance runners, gymnasts, figure skaters and ballet dancers, but can affect recreational women athletes who run as little as 12 miles per week. These women usually have low body weight, disordered eating behaviors and poor nutrition (low calorie, fat, and protein intake).

There are several health consequences of amenorrhea. For example, infertility is possible. Unfavorable changes in lipoprotein profiles increase the chance of a woman to develop coronary artery disease. Low estrogen levels can lead to increased loss of bone mineral density, which increases the risk of fractures.

Osteoporosis

More than 25 million Americans (mostly women) suffer from osteoporosis, premature bone loss and/or inadequate bone formation resulting in low bone mass and increased skeletal fragility and risk of fracture. After the age of 35, all humans incur some small loss of bone mass each year. Most people in industrialized countries have some degree of lowered bone mass, also known as osteopenia. Bone density is affected by a number of factors, including genetics, nutrition (adequate calcium intake of 1500 mg per day), mechanical loading (resistance training), achieving peak bone mass during adolescence, and menstrual history. Furthermore, if a woman is childless, has experienced premature menopause or suffered from prolonged premenopausal amenorrhea, she has a higher risk of osteoporosis. Other factors that increase an individual's risk are family history, low estrogen levels, low calcium intake, sedentary lifestyle, low body weight, high fiber intake, excessive tobacco, alcohol or caffeine use, excessive protein intake, and prolonged corticosteroid use.

Fortunately, in most cases, osteoporosis is preventable and treatable. Calcium is the single most important dietary factor in preventing osteoporosis. Regular exercise can slow down and perhaps even halt age-related loss of bone mass or could delay its progression. Individuals are more likely to experience absolute gains in bone mass through resistance training than with aerobic exercise. For optimal bone health, women should engage in physical activity starting at an early age in order to attain as high a bone mineral content as possible.

Menopause

Menopause is the point in time when menstrual function ceases. Menopause occurs when a woman stops menstruating for 12 months (i.e., her ovaries stop producing estrogen, progesterone and testosterone hormones). The average age for the onset of menopause is 51, but it can happen in a woman's 30s or even 60s. This event also marks the end of a woman's reproductive years.

Among the typical symptoms of menopause are hot flashes, night sweats, insomnia, fatigue, depression, irritability, heart palpitations, joint pain, reproductive tract

For optimal bone health, women should engage in physical activity starting at an early age in order to attain as high a bone mineral content as possible.

changes and weight gain in the abdominal area. With the onset of menopause, some related health concerns (heart disease and osteoporosis) may occur. A woman may also experience a variety of uncomfortable symptoms, most of which can be alleviated by regular exercise.

For example, aerobic exercise can lead to improved mood, stress relief, abdominal fat loss, and improved quality of sleep. Resistance training can increase bone mass, while basic physical activity can elevate a woman's estrogen level—both of which will reduce a woman's susceptibility to osteoporosis.

Premenstrual Syndrome (PMS)

Premenstrual syndrome is a type of menstrual problem that is caused by a hormonal imbalance that occurs a few days prior to the start of a woman's menstrual cycle. It can manifest itself emotionally, behaviorally, and physically. Severe PMS can be alleviated with medication prescribed by a physician. Exercise has also been shown to reduce PMS symptoms. Among the other steps that a woman can take to help her relieve her PMS symptoms include stopping smoking, losing weight, reducing the stress in her life, decreasing her intake of alcohol, and eating a diet low in sodium and sugar.

Musculoskeletal Concerns

Although injuries appear to be sports specific—rather than gender specific, certain women are particularly susceptible to stress fractures. Among the factors that increase a woman's risk of suffering stress fractures are low calcium intake, low estrogen levels, amenorrhea, and anorexia nervosa. Eating a well-balanced diet and not over-exercising will help her reduce her level of risk.

Most women are also more susceptible to kneecap pain than men (because of the angular alignment of a woman's pelvis and thigh muscles with her knee). Kneecap pain is more prevalent in women because of their wider hips and pelvises which draw the kneecap toward the outside of the joint putting excessive pressure on the underside of the kneecap. Sitting for prolonged periods can worsen the pain. Exercises that put excessive pressure on the knee should be avoided, such as squats, leg extensions, and walking down a slope or stairs. Emphasis should be put on strengthening and stretching the quadriceps (muscles in the front of the thigh).

Breast Protection While Exercising

Proper breast support while exercising is also an important issue for women to consider. Because a woman's breasts are composed mainly of fat and supported only by skin and connective tissue, wearing a good sports bra is very important. The most important factor is to wear something that is comfortable. Among the essential components of a good sports bra are seamless cups; wide, non-elastic straps; breathable fabrics; and covered hooks and fasteners.

Pre and Postnatal Physical Activity

Until recently, many pregnant women have been hesitant to continue exercising because of the variety of opinions concerning whether the practice was safe. However, considerable evidence supports the fact that properly performed and monitored exercise imposes little risk to either the mother or her fetus. In fact, prenatal exercise provides several benefits to a pregnant woman. In a similar vein, most experts recommend that a woman should resume her exercise efforts as soon as feasible after giving birth.

Yes, She Should

Exercise can and should be an integral part of a woman's lifestyle. It should be a core element of her commitment to total fitness. In that regard, a woman's exercise program should take certain gender-related issue into account in order to make her exercise efforts as productive and safe as possible. As such, sound exercise is not and must not be perceived as an activity for men only.

CHAPTER FOURTEEN

EXERCISE AND AGING

It's never too late to start exercising.

Aging involves at least three truths. The first truth is that everybody does it. The second truth is that everybody does it differently. In other words, a typical older adult does not exist. Third, there can be a clear difference between chronological "old" and physiological "old". For the purposes of this book, at You Turn, we do not wish to establish one standard age defined as "old", rather we feel each individual should be evaluated and guided to their individual abilities.

The point to keep in mind is that every species on earth (e.g., humans, dogs, elephants, plants, etc.) has a distinct lifespan. Generic man, for example, has a lifespan that is approximately 100 years. As such, most of the research on aging has focused on the issue of how the quality of life can be improved for you up to the point where your life ends.

Empirical evidence and observations suggest that age is primarily a function of how well you do things physically. As such, you become old when you no longer are able to perform the basic physical tasks in your life. The fundamental issue to be addressed, then, is what functional effects does aging have on your body and what (if anything) can you do about it.

The Effects of Aging on Your Body

As you age, the various systems of your body tend to undergo several changes. Collectively, these changes can result in a gradual decline in your ability to perform the basic activities of daily living. For example, your cardiovascular system experiences a number of relatively prominent changes as you age, including the following:

- A decrease in both the amount of cardiac muscle you have and the volume of blood your heart can process per beat, which decreases your heart's ability to pump blood.

- A decrease in the level of nerve activity to your heart, which results in a less powerful heart contraction and a lower attainable maximal heart rate.

- A decrease in the elasticity of your major blood vessels, which results in an elevated blood pressure level (both at rest and during physical activity).

Aging also affects your pulmonary system in some major ways. For example, the functional unit of your lungs (the alveoli) loses some of its structural integrity, resulting in less available surface area for the essential exchange of gas, thereby limiting the amount of oxygen your body will allow to enter your blood stream. The energy cost of breathing also increases as a person ages because an individual's lung tissues become less elastic, respiratory muscles become less strong, and rib cage muscles become more stiff.

Aging is also associated with numerous changes in your musculoskeletal system. For example, as you age, you tend to suffer from a progressive, steady decline in both muscle mass and muscular fitness, leading to deficiencies in gait and balance, a loss of functional mobility, an increased risk of falling, and, ultimately, a loss of independence.

Furthermore, your muscles undergo specific chemical changes that decrease the ability of your muscles to extract oxygen from your blood. In addition, older people are at a higher risk for osteoporosis and bone fractures that result from a decrease in bone mineral content and mass that is associated with aging. An increased level of stiffness of the connective tissues in your body's joints that results in a loss of joint flexibility and mobility is also attributed to aging.

Fortunately, a significant portion (some estimates have been as high as 50%) of the system-wide physiological decline typically seen with aging can be attributed to the "disuse syndrome." More simply stated, **much of the functional decline associated with the so-called "aging process" is due to the fact that as people get older, they become less physically active.** As such, considerable evidence supports the conclusion that to a point, the more physically active you are, the more slowly you "age."

Effects of Exercise on Slowing Down the Aging Process

A critical question concerning the aging process involves whether exercise can slow down the biological changes that occur over the course of your lifetime. The answer appears to be a resounding "yes," although the extent to which exercising on a regular basis can affect the response of certain bodily systems to aging is generally unknown. At the least, a physically active lifestyle can positively affect age-associated declines that in large part may be attributed to the fact that most people become less active as they age.

Cardiorespiratory Adaptations

Numerous studies have shown that elderly individuals who exercise can achieve a demonstrable cardiorespiratory training effect. For example, even though the ability to consume oxygen declines in everyone as they get older, physically active individuals are able to slow their average rate of decline in this consumption level to a level approximately half that of their sedentary counterparts. This means that an active 65-year-old person can be as aerobically fit as a 45-year-old sedentary person. In addition, older individuals who remain physically active do not experience the typical rise in blood pressure that occurs with aging.

Musculoskeletal Adaptations

Considerable evidence supports the belief that strength training can forestall the rate of deterioration of the musculoskeletal system in older persons. Older individuals who engaged in a resistance training program have been able to maintain their strength. In fact, their strength levels actually increased dramatically. In comparison, inactive individuals typically show a 20-30% loss in strength by age 65. Participants in experimental research that has been conducted on the effect of resistance training or older adults have also incurred an increase in muscle mass, in contrast to the decrease that traditionally occurs in their inactive counterparts. Finally, proper strength training has been documented to maintain or increase joint flexibility, since it involves having an individual exercise through a full range of motion.

Body Composition Adaptations

Exercise can reduce the accumulation of body fat that accompanies aging and can slow, if not reverse, the substantial loss of fat-free mass that usually goes hand-in-hand with the increase in body fat. Older people can maintain the level of body fat that they had in their youth if they remain consistently physically active and maintain an appropriate diet throughout their lives. Researchers suggest that proper strength training can limit (if not reverse) the loss of lean muscle mass levels that often accompanies aging.

Developing an Appropriate Exercise Prescription

The general principles of exercise prescription apply to individuals of all ages. However, the wide range of health and fitness levels observed among older adults makes prescribing exercise for them more difficult. Accordingly, great care must be taken in establishing the type, intensity, duration, and frequency of exercise. Common sense suggests that older adults should perform aerobic exercise, resistance training, flexibility exercise, and balance training on a regular basis.

Prescribing Aerobic Exercise

As previously discussed, older adults can benefit by engaging in aerobic exercise. With a few age-related adjustments, the guidelines for prescribing aerobic exercise for older adults are generally similar to those used for their younger counterparts.

Type

Selecting a mode of exercise for developing aerobic fitness can involve several factors. For most older persons (particularly those who have been sedentary), the exercise mode should be one that does not impose significant orthopedic stress on the aged musculoskeletal system. Among the more popular methods of exercising that older adults use to develop aerobic fitness are the following:

- Walking: Walking is an excellent form of exercise for young and old alike. It is beneficial for older adults for several reasons: it doesn't require learning a new skill;

Considerable evidence supports the conclusion that to a point, the more physically active you are, the more slowly you "age."

it can be done almost anywhere, indoors or outdoors; it doesn't require special clothing or equipment, except for a good pair of walking shoes; and, finally, if performed on a treadmill, it can be an activity in which preselected and performance measures can be monitored by the person or an exercise specialist. The primary disadvantage of walking is the fact that a certain amount of orthopedic stress is imposed on the skeletal joints of the user.

- Water Exercise: Swimming and water aerobic exercise (aquatic) classes offer certain advantages for older adults. The benefit most frequently cited is the fact that water-based activities have lower musculoskeletal injury rates and greater joint range of motion than most traditional weight-bearing activities. In addition, exercising in water offers the opportunity to engage in both upper and lower body muscular resistance exercise. The most obvious downside of water-based activities involves the need for access to a pool and the fact that an individual may not feel comfortable around water. Also, aquatic exercise classes do not promote positive bone adaptations since water-based activities are not weight-bearing.

- Stationary Cycling: Stationary cycling is a particularly safe exercise for older adults. The weather is not a factor indoors. No substantial concern exists that an older adult might fall off the cycle. If adapting to the seat is a problem, equipping the cycle with an extra large seat tends to minimize the discomfort for people unaccustomed to a bicycle seat. If excessive fatigue in the user's thigh muscles is a problem (given the role of the quadriceps in exercise cycling), gradually increasing the exercise duration while reducing or holding intensity (i.e., pedal resistance) constant may minimize the problem. The aerobic portion of the cycling exercise session may be broken into 10-minute segments and interspersed with 10-minute bouts of other forms of aerobic exercise, such as walking, simulated stair climbing, etc. Stationary cycling has at least two significant shortcomings. First, an exercise cycle is needed. A quality exercise cycle can either be purchased or be part of the equipment offering of a health-fitness facility. Second, and more importantly, as a non-weight-bearing activity, exercise cycling does not offer the beneficial effects on bone mass that weight-bearing activity does.

- Aerobic Dance: Aerobic dance has several significant advantages and disadvantages for the older population. The advantages include the following: aerobic dance sessions are structured, yet social, events; aerobic dance can improve body awareness and can approximate everyday motions such as bending and reaching; aerobic dance exercise provides an opportunity to work on posture, gait and balance; and, finally, aerobic dance enables exercises involving coordination and flexibility to be integrated effectively with aerobic fitness activities. Among the more important possible disadvantages of this form of exercise are the following: an aerobic dance class must comprise persons with similar capabilities (to ensure safety); the risk of acute or chronic injuries is high; and the fitness benefits from class to class are not as predictable as from more structured forms of aerobic exercise (e.g., cycling, stair climbing, etc.). Finally, aerobic dance is more dependent than other forms of aerobic exercise on the skills of the exercise leader for direction, safety, motivation, and ultimate effectiveness.

Intensity

Perhaps the most important and, at the same time, potentially the most problematic training variable is exercise intensity. Exercise intensity must be sufficient to stress (overload) the cardiovascular, pulmonary, and musculoskeletal systems without overtasking them. In general, the intensity of exercise coincides with the training heart rate. Training heart rate (THR) is often determined by taking a straight percentage of age-predicted maximal heart rate (i.e., 220 minus age). This method of defining exercise intensity can, however, be very misleading in older individuals. A high level of variability exists for maximal heart rates in person over 55 years of age (maximal heart rates can range from as low as 100 bpm to as high as 190 bpm). As a result, training heart rates calculated on the basis of age-predicted maximal heart rates can either underestimate or overestimate the exercise intensity. Thus, it is always better to use an accurate measurement maximal heart rate (MHR) rather than age-predicted MHR.

The recommended level of exercise intensity for an older adult is 50 to 70 % of maximal heart rate. Since many older persons suffer from a variety of medical conditions, a conservative approach to prescribing aerobic exercises is usually warranted. Individuals with a relatively low level of functional capacity should initially engage in aerobic exercise at an intensity range of 50 to 60 % of maximal HR, which can then be very gradually increased over a period of two to three months. When setting exercise intensity for older individuals, the general rule is "start low and go slow."

Duration

Exercise duration and intensity go hand and hand. An increase in one often requires a decrease in the other. The prescription for duration is usually expressed in terms of time, distance, or calories. All three are interrelated. Most people prefer, however, to use time as their indicator of duration because of its comparative simplicity of use. Other than a watch or access to a clock, nothing is required except the ability to tell time.

The ACSM guideline (aimed at primarily healthy younger to middle-aged adults) for duration recommends that an aerobic exercise workout take between 20 and 60 minutes. The goal of most older adults should initially be 20 to 30 minutes of sustained activity, although this number could range from 10 – 60 minutes depending upon their level of daily activity. During the initial stages of an exercise program, however, some older adults may have difficulty sustaining aerobic exercise for more than 10 minutes. For such individuals one viable option may be to perform the exercise in several 10-minute bouts throughout the day. If the exercise session is segmented, the individual should be encouraged to perform it at regularly scheduled times, so as to enhance compliance and adherence. For individuals with a low functional capacity, it may actually be preferable to schedule frequent 10-minute bouts of exercise throughout the day. Whatever their fitness level, however, to avoid injury and ensure safety, older individuals should raise the difficulty level of their workouts primarily through increases in exercise duration.

Frequency

Similar to other age groups, research shows that older adults need to exercise aerobically 3-5 days a week in order to achieve the intended training effect. Exercising less than twice a week has been found to produce little or no meaningful training response. By the same token, exercising more than 5 days a week results in little or no further improvement in an individual's ability to consume oxygen. In fact, the amount of positive change in a person's aerobic fitness level begins to plateau when the individual exercises more than 3 to 4 days per week. During the initial stages of weight-bearing aerobic exercise, exercising on alternate days is recommended to gradually give the individual's body an opportunity to adapt to the stresses being imposed upon it (thereby reducing the likelihood of an "overuse" injury). People who want to exercise aerobically on a daily basis, should alternate between weight-bearing (e.g., walking or stair climbing) and non-weight-bearing exercises (e.g., exercise cycling).

Prescribing Resistance Training

The effects of resistance training and various strength training protocols have been relatively well-documented for younger populations. Recently published research findings suggest that muscular fitness (muscular strength and muscular endurance) also offers considerable benefits to older adults. For example, it appears that strength training may enable elderly individuals (particularly women) to be able to perform their daily living tasks with greater ease, as well as leading to a heightened sense of self-confidence and self-worth. A certain level of muscular fitness is critical for individuals to retain their independence. Individuals obviously want and need to perform certain daily tasks for themselves. It is believed that strength training provides significant skeletal benefits for men and women of all ages. While the thought of "pumping up" to older adults might seem somewhat strange, it appears to be an inescapable fact that an appropriate level of muscular fitness is integral to ensuring that individuals are able to spend their latter years in a self-functioning, dignified manner.

Although the ability of older adults to realize significant strength gains has been documented, the specifics of resistance training prescriptions for older adults have not been adequately addressed. For example, a number of studies have shown that achieving a training effect for muscular fitness does not have to involve extended periods of time in the weight room, lifting massive amounts of free weights. On the contrary, calisthenics using body weight to stimulate an overload of the muscle, weighted and non-weighted stair climbing, and weight machines have all been found to produce substantial increases in muscular fitness.

Similar to aerobic fitness, the ACSM has developed recommendations concerning what constitutes an appropriate resistance training protocol. Adhering to these guidelines can help ensure that the strength training efforts of older adults are both safe and productive.

Intensity

The ACSM recommends that, at a minimum, an individual should perform one set of 8 to 10 exercises that train the major muscle groups. Each set should involve 10 to 15 repetitions that elicit a perceived exertion rating of 12-13 (somewhat hard). The selection of exercises should ensure that all of the major muscle groups in the body are included in the training session. Depending on an individual's personal philosophy, additional sets could be performed. Most research, however, suggests that additional sets may have limited value at best.

Frequency

The ACSM recommends that resistance training be performed at least twice a week, with at least 48 hours of rest between workouts. Research indicates that as an individual becomes older, the need for sufficient time to recover from the resistance stress imposed upon the body increases.

Duration

The ACSM suggests that resistance training sessions lasting longer than 60 minutes may have a detrimental effect on an individual's level of exercise adherence. Adherence to the guidelines of the ACSM would permit individuals to complete total body strength training sessions within 20 –25 minutes.

Basic Strength Training Guidelines

Regardless of which specific protocol you might adopt as you age, several common sense guidelines pertaining to resistance training should be followed:

- Focus the major goal of your resistance-training program on developing sufficient muscle fitness to enhance your ability to live a physically independent lifestyle.

- Have your first several resistance-training sessions closely supervised and monitored by trained personnel who are sensitive to your special needs and capabilities (as an older adult).

- Start out (the first 8 weeks) with very minimal levels of resistance to allow for adaptations of your connective tissue elements.

- Learn the proper training techniques for all of the exercises to be used in your program.

- Maintain your normal breathing patterns while exercising, since breath holding can cause your blood pressure to rise excessively.

- As a training effect occurs, achieve an overload initially by increasing the number of repetitions of a given exercise you perform and then by increasing the absolute amount of resistance you lift during a particular exercise.

- Never use a resistance that is so heavy that you cannot perform at least eight repetitions per set. Heavy resistances can be potentially dangerous and damaging to your skeletal and joint structures.

- Perform all exercises in a manner in which the speed is controlled. In order to prevent orthopedic trauma to your joint structures, avoid ballistic (fast and jerky) movements. Lift and lower all weights in a slow, controlled manner.

- Perform the exercises in a range of motion that is within a "pain free arc" (i.e., the maximum range of motion which does not elicit pain or discomfort) for you. As positive adaptations occur, gradually increase your exercise range of motion in order to improve your level of flexibility.

- Perform multi-joint exercises (as opposed to single-joint exercises) since they tend to help you develop functional muscular fitness.

- Given a choice, use machines to resistance train, as opposed to free weights. The primary advantages of machines are that they tend to require less skill to use, they protect your back by stabilizing your body position, and they allow you to start with lower resistances, to increase by smaller increments (this is not true for all strength training machines), and to more easily control your exercise range of motion.

- Don't overtrain. Two strength training sessions per week are the minimum number required to produce positive adaptations. Depending on the circumstances, more sessions may neither be desirable nor productive.

- If you suffer from arthritis, don't participate in strength training during active periods of pain or inflammation, since exercise could exacerbate your condition.

- Engage in a year-round resistance-training program on a regular basis, since it has been shown that the cessation of resistance training can result in a rapid significant loss of strength. When returning from a lay-off, resume strength training with resistances that are equivalent to or less than 50 percent of the intensity at which you had been training before, and then gradually increase the level of resistance.

Prescribing Flexibility Exercises

An adequate range of motion in all of the joints of the body is important to maintaining an acceptable level of musculoskeletal function. Unfortunately, efforts to identify the most effective protocol for developing flexibility have been somewhat limited, particularly in comparison to the other basic components of physical fitness. What is almost universally accepted, but not documented, is the fact that maintaining adequate levels of flexibility will enhance functional capabilities (e.g., bending and twisting) and reduce injury potential (e.g., risk of muscle strains and low back problems)—particularly for the aged. A well-rounded program of stretching has been shown to counteract the usual decline or improve flexibility in the elderly. As such, it is critical that you include a sound stretching program as part of your regimen as you age.

Intensity

The ACSM recommends stretching exercises involving a slow dynamic movement, followed by a static stretch that is sustained for 10 to 30 seconds. You should perform stretching exercises for every major joint (hip, back, shoulder, knee, upper trunk, and neck regions) in your body. Three to five repetitions of each exercise should be done. The degree of stretch achieved should not be to the point of substantial pain.

Frequency

The ACSM recommends that stretching exercises should be performed at least 3 times a week. In reality, stretching exercises should be included as an integral part of the warm-up and cool-down exercises that you should perform prior to and at the conclusion of all of your exercise workouts regardless of your age. Individuals can, however, choose to devote an entire exercise session to flexibility. This can be particularly appropriate for deconditioned older adults who are beginning an exercise program.

Duration

The stretching phase of your exercise session should involve approximately 5 to 10 minutes collectively each workout. Several common sense guidelines pertaining to stretching by older adults should be followed:

- Always precede stretching exercises with some type of warm-up activity to increase heart rate and internal body temperature. It is safer and more productive to stretch a warm muscle.

- Stretch smoothly and never bounce. When you bounce while stretching, you cause your muscles to tighten to protect themselves—this factor actually inhibits effective muscle stretching. Moreover, ballistic (i.e., bouncing) movements can cause the very sort of muscle tears that stretching is designed to prevent.

- Do not stretch a joint beyond its range of motion. Tissue has a failure point. It is important to remember that wide variations in range of motion exist between individuals.

- Gradually ease into a stretch, and hold it only as long as it feels comfortable. If you stretch to the point of feeling extreme pain, you increase your likelihood of being injured.

Balance Training

A great proportion, possibly up to 50% of older persons, report some difficulty with maintaining balance. Falls are the most evident by-product of a diminished level of balance. Poor balance is caused by the interaction of a number of factors, some of which can be mitigated by participating regularly in an exercise program. Accordingly, no later than at 70 years of age, individuals should be encouraged to include a balance training program into their regular exercise regimen.

Several different types of exercise activities can be used to develop better balance. Perhaps the simplest technique to learn (the flamingo exercise) involves standing on one leg, then alternating to the other leg. The one-legged stance position should be maintained for 30 seconds on each leg for a total duration of 5 minutes. The ultimate goal is to be able to do this with your eyes closed. If this is not possible, keep your eyes open. If you still have difficulty performing the flamingo, hold onto the back of a chair with one finger, one hand, or both hands, depending on your degree of unsteadiness, eventually progressing to being able to stand on one leg with your eyes closed. Another basic balance exercise involves walking heel to toe in a straight line forward and backward. Yet another balance exercise involves writing the alphabet with the foot of one leg, while balancing on the opposite leg. One final exercise for developing balance involves standing near a wall and practicing leaning toward it in each direction. Any or all of these balance techniques have been shown to result in up to a 50 percent improvement in balance among older adults.

Making Sure That It is Safe to Exercise

If you are an older adult, you must take steps to ensure that it is medically safe for you to exercise. This factor involves seeing a physician and undergoing a physical examination and evaluation before you start an exercise program. The extent of the evaluation depends on your age and health status. Men over 40, women over 50, and all individuals at high risk (e.g., having one or more of the following risk factors— smoking, hypertension, high blood cholesterol, obesity, stress, family history of medical problems, diabetes) are strongly encouraged to undergo a physician-supervised, graded exercise test.

A safety-oriented exercise program also involves starting at a level of intensity appropriate for you and then progressing gradually. The temptation to do too much too soon should be avoided. Moderation is essential. A major cause of musculoskeletal injuries is overuse—placing demands on your body that your body simply is not capable of handling. A sound exercise program always includes provisions for stretching the major joints of your body before and after exercising. It also ensures that you get proper rest along with exercise. Rest enables you to recover from the demands placed on your body by exercise.

The final step is for you to be sure to listen to your body. You must respond to specific warning signals of exertion intolerance. These warning signs are grouped into three general categories, according to their severity.

Category I: If you experience any of the following symptoms, you should stop exercising immediately and consult a physician before resuming exercise:

- Abnormal heart rhythm (irregular pulse, fluttering, pumping or palpitations in your chest or throat, a sudden burst of rapid heart beats, or a very sudden slowing of the pulse).

- Pain or pressure in your arm or throat or in the middle of your chest (either during or after exercising).

- Acute heat or overuse-related signals (dizziness; light-headedness; sudden loss of coordination; mental disorientation; profuse sweating; glassy stare; unnatural pallor; blueness; fainting).

Category II: If you experience any of the following symptoms and the suggested (listed) remedy doesn't work for you, you should see a physician before exercising again:

- Persistent rapid heart rate (remedy—keep your heart rate at the lower end of your aerobic training zone for several minutes at the start of your exercise session, and then increase it very slowly as you continue to exercise).

- Flare-up of musculoskeletal conditions, such as osteoarthritis (remedy—stop exercising until the condition subsides; you should take your normal medicine for any such condition).

- Nausea after exercising (remedy—reduce the intensity level of both your present and future exercise bouts; take a more gradual cooling-down period after exercising).

- Extreme breathlessness that lasts more than 10 minutes after you have stopped exercising (remedy—never exercise to the point where you're too breathless to talk while you're exercising).

Category III: The following warning signs can usually be handled without your consulting a physician:

- Insomnia (remedy—exercise at the lower end of your aerobic training zone for the next several exercise bouts, and then begin gradually to increase the intensity level at which you exercise).

- Side-stitch (remedy—sit, lean forward, and attempt to push your abdominal organs against your diaphragm).

The Effects of Exercise on the Lifestyle

Exercise on a regular basis can have a positive effect on the overall quality of life in older adults in many ways, including the following:

- Regular exercise can provide older individuals with the functional capacity necessary to perform basic living tasks, such as shopping, ambulation, personal care, and cooking meals.

- Physical activity can help an older person adapt to the changing social roles that sometimes accompany advancing age. For example, a physical activity-based program may replace work in the life of the individual.

- Social interaction can be promoted through exercise programs. Physical activity can help in adjusting to a traumatic event—e.g., retirement, the death of a loved one—by providing an avenue for social interaction and combating feelings of depression.

- Regular exercise can assist individuals in adjusting to retirement. Exercise, for example, can provide a relatively inexpensive activity for those on a reduced income. In addition, maintaining physical fitness enables older persons to remain independent, thereby incurring fewer of the costs for assistance that arise if they need home management and personal care.

- Old age frequently requires that older people must scale down their housing or move into an apartment or retirement community. Since many retirement communities do not take people who are physically dependent, maintaining physical fitness enables individuals to have more diverse options in their possible physical living arrangements. In several multi-level retirement communities, for example, the average cost for assisted living (e.g., help in making the bed, meals, home finances) is estimated to be more than double the monthly average cost required to live independently.

Living Smart

Depending on your point of reference, reflecting on the aging process may present a rather dismal picture. In fact, a generation ago much confusion and fatalism existed regarding aging. Old age was viewed as the time of inevitable and irretrievable decline. By no means, however, is the future as bleak as it might first appear. With respect to the effects of the aging process, to a great extent, you can control your own destiny. Regular exercise can and does slow down many of the debilitating effects of advancing years. The basic guideline with regard to exercise and aging is that it is never too late to start. It is not "you're too old to exercise," it is "you're too old not to exercise." Irrefutable evidence exists to support the fact that mixing strict adherence to sound exercise principles with a personal commitment to common sense and patience could well serve as an appropriate recipe for improving and sustaining an independent lifestyle for the elderly. In other words, "living smart" is the fundamental priority for "living well"… at any age.

CHAPTER FIFTEEN

EXERCISE AND THE

ENVIRONMENT

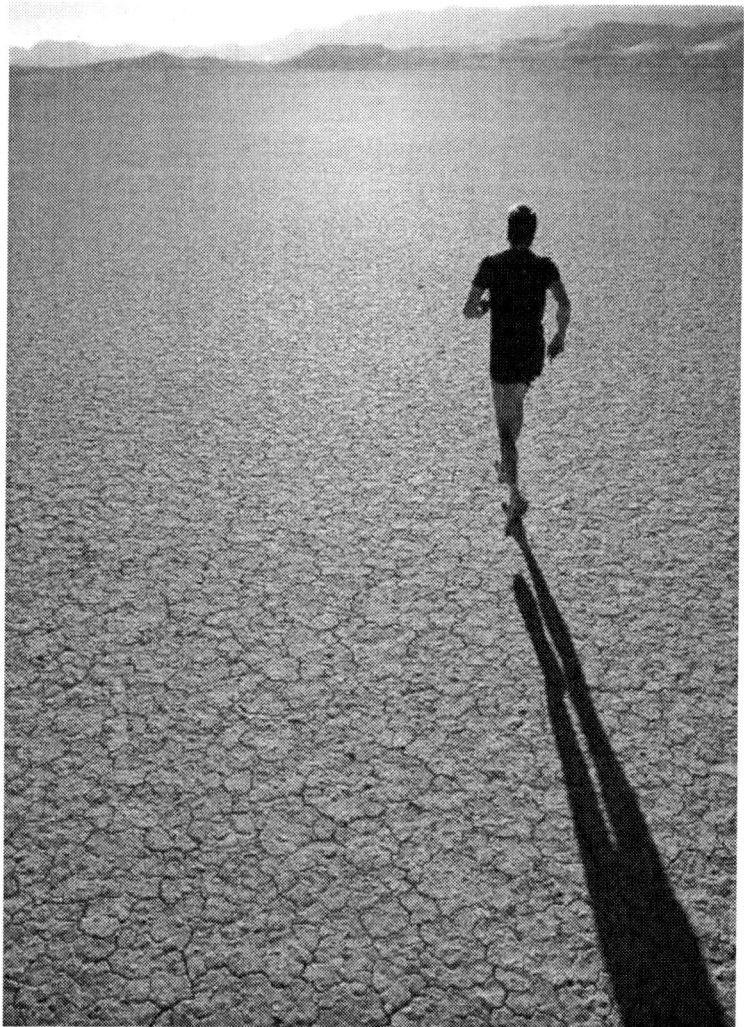

Understanding how your body responds to a variety of environmental conditions that can be present during exercise is critical to ensuring that you remain safe when you engage in physical activity.

As a human being, your body is extremely adaptable to a variety of environments. You are able to tolerate and exercise, to a point, in a diverse array of environmental conditions—heat, cold, high altitudes, and even air pollution. Each of these conditions imposes certain negative demands on the systems of our body—particularly your cardiovascular, respiratory, renal, muscular, and neural systems.

Exercising in the Heat

Understanding how your body responds to a variety of environmental conditions that can be present during exercise is critical to ensuring that you remain safe when you engage in physical activity. Of the many environmental factors that can have an impact on your opportunity to engage in safe and effective exercise, none is as potentially life —and health—threatening as heat stress. During the hot and often humid conditions of the summer, heat stress can pose a real threat for those individuals who choose to engage in aerobic exercise activities—either outdoors, or indoors in facilities without adequate air cooling systems.

Exercise and Heat Balance

When you are at rest, your body has little or no trouble losing enough heat to maintain a steady body temperature. Your body rids itself of excess heat by sweating, by exhaling air warmed in the lungs, and by redirecting blood flow to the skin. The combination of hot weather and exercise can overload these mechanisms. When you start to exercise, heat is produced more rapidly than it can be dissipated by your body. Therefore, maintaining your body temperature within safe limits becomes more difficult. When you exercise in a cool environment, your body is able to lose heat by means of radiation/convection via air movement around your body and evaporative heat loss from sweating. Sustained exercise in a hot/humid environment, however, makes it extremely difficult for you to maintain normal body temperature and fluid balance. High heat and humidity impair your body's ability to lose heat by radiation/convection and evaporation, respectively. This inability to lose heat during exercise in a hot/humid environment results in an elevated body temperature and a greatly increased sweat rate (and concomitantly greater fluid loss) when compared to similar amounts of exercise performed in a cool environment. Several detrimental side effects can occur as a result of having an elevated body core temperature and suffering excessive fluid losses. At the least, your performance capability in endurance activities can be diminished; at the worst, you will develop a heat injury.

Heat Injuries

A heat injury can occur whenever the demands of the environment and/or the exercise exceed the capabilities of your body's thermoregulatory (body temperature-controlling) mechanisms. Two primary causes of heat injuries are dehydration (excessive body fluid loss) and hyperthermia (high internal body temperatures). The three most common types of heat injuries are heat cramps, heat exhaustion, and heat stroke.

Heat cramps are an initial sign of heat injury. They are characterized by involuntary cramping and spasm in the muscle groups used during the exercise. They generally result from excessive fluid and electrolyte (sodium and potassium) loss. An individual experiencing heat cramps will sometimes complain of headaches, dizziness, and nausea. Research suggests that in most instances, drinking adequate amounts of fluid before, during, and after exercising can help to prevent (and treat) this condition.

Heat exhaustion—a more serious form of heat injury—is characterized by the presence of several of the following symptoms: a rapid, weak pulse; profuse sweating; paleness; cold, clammy skin; dizziness; palpitations; nausea; headaches; shallow breathing; diarrhea; and cramps. It results from an acute (sudden) fluid loss in the body and the inability of your circulatory system to adjust for the compensatory vasodilation that occurs in your skin and active muscles. The standard treatment of heat exhaustion includes supine rest in a cool area and ingesting plenty of fluids. Most individuals feel better within a few hours after treatment.

Heat stroke is the most serious of the various types of heat injuries and represents a major medical emergency. Heat strokes may appear either suddenly or gradually. The major symptoms of heat stoke include extreme body heat (temperature as high as 106∞F); hot, dry skin; bright red or flushed skin color; confusion; headache; sensitivity to light; little or no sweating; strong, rapid pulse; dilated pupils; unconsciousness; labored breathing; and possible convulsions. Heat strokes are caused primarily by a failure of the body's thermoregulatory system to trigger the sweating mechanism, resulting in an explosive increase in the body's core temperature due to insufficient, evaporative cooling. Doctors treat heat stroke by administering fluids intravenously and rapidly cooling the body. People die with heat stroke. Seek medical attention immediately!

Avoiding Heat Injury

By adhering to the following basic guidelines you can avoid sustaining a heat injury:

- Make sure that you are adequately hydrated. This can be accomplished by consuming large amounts of fluid (just short of feeling bloated) thirty minutes before exercise, drinking at least six ounces of fluid while exercising after every 20 minutes of exercise, and drinking beyond the point of where you feel thirsty during the recovery period. Water is generally considered to be the best hydration fluid unless your duration of exercise exceeds 90 minutes. If so, diluted commercial drinks containing carbohydrates may be beneficial.

- Beverages containing caffeine or alcohol should be avoided, since they promote fluid loss through urine.

- Become acclimatized to the environment. Acclimatization, your body's gradual (it usually takes 10-14 days of heat exposure combined with exercise) adaptation to changes in environment, can greatly reduce your risk for heat injury. Once you've become acclimatized, you'll sweat sooner, produce more sweat, and lose fewer electrolytes in your sweat. The net effects of acclimatization are a lower body core temperature, a decreased heart rate response to exercise, and a diminished potential for electrolyte depletion.

- Lower your exercise intensity (especially during the acclimatization period) because this will decrease the exercise-induced heat load and, as a result, reduce the strain on your thermoregulatory mechanisms.

- Wear loose-fitting, lightweight clothing that permits air currents to circulate around your body and allows you to expose as much skin as possible to increase the available surface area for sweat evaporation to occur. Light colors are recommended since they reflect rather than absorb radiant heat from the sun's rays.

- Never wear clothing that is impermeable to water (e.g., rubberized sweat suits), since such clothing prevents the evaporation of sweat from your skin and thereby increases your risk of heat injury.

- Respect the environmental conditions since temperature and relative humidity can greatly influence both the degree of heat stress and your body's ability to effectively respond to the heat stress. As a general rule of thumb, you should consider curtailing exercise when the temperature is above 90∞F, and concurrently, the relative humidity is above 60 percent.

- Stop exercising immediately if you develop any sign or symptom of heat injury.

Keeping Cool

The risks of heat injuries are not so great that you should not take full advantage of a regular program of aerobic exercise during the summer months. They should not be ignored, however. You need to respect the environment and adjust your exercise program accordingly. You can beat the heat by being smart. The key to exercising safely in a hot environment is to be prepared. Drink up, slow down, and have fun exercising this summer.

Exercising in the Cold

The winter season signals the coming of cold weather for a significant portion of the United States. Cold weather, however, should not necessarily preclude you from engaging in aerobic exercise out-of-doors. You can safely exercise in the cold provided

You need to respect the environment and adjust your exercise program accordingly.

that your follow certain common sense guidelines. These guidelines fully apply to all options for exercising aerobically outdoors in the cold, including jogging, cross-country skiing, ice skating, etc.

Fortunately, under most conditions, it will not be too cold for you to safely exercise outdoors provided that you take appropriate precautionary measures. In a few instances, however, the effective temperature may drop to a level that could place you at risk for a cold injury if you exercised outdoors. The wind chill index is the most common way to express the effective temperature. Because wind accelerates heat loss by increasing the degree to which the warmer insulating air layer which surrounds your body is constantly being replaced by the cooler ambient air, wind can cause significant cooling of your body. For example, the combination of a 20°F temperature with 20 mile per hour winds produces an effective temperature of -10°F. If you plan to exercise in cold weather, you should review a wind chill index table to ensure that the cooling effect of the wind—combined with the ambient temperature—does not place you in a potentially threatening cold stress environment. As a basic rule of thumb, any effective wind-chill temperature colder than -10°F should be viewed as being a risky environment in which to exercise.

Cold Hands, Warm Heart

Before you begin to consider what you can do to battle cold weather conditions, you need first to understand how your body responds to the cold. The two primary ways your body physiologically responds to the cold is to increase its metabolic rate and its degree of tissue insulation.

Changes in metabolic rate can be elicited either voluntarily or involuntarily. Your body's metabolic rate is increased voluntarily by exercising, and involuntarily as a result of shivering thermogenesis. Thermogenesis involves the production of body heat by means of shivering (and to a smaller degree, sympathetic and/or hormonally induced chemical excitation). Shivering occurs when "cold" signals to the hypothalamus in your brain trigger the release of nonrhythmic impulses to the anterior motoneurons of the skeletal muscles throughout your body. Contrary to your perception of the process of shivering, these impulses do not cause your muscles to actually shake. Instead, they prompt the muscle to oscillate. Involuntary muscle shivering can increase the amount of heat your body produces to go as high as four to five times normal.

Your body's initial response to the cold, however, is to constrict blood vessels. With the exception of your cranial (head) region, this vasoconstriction occurs in the peripheral (surface) blood vessels of your body. Blood is literally redirected from the surface areas of your body into the deeper blood vessels, the net effect of this process of vasoconstriction is to increase the relative insulative level of your surface tissues. When blood is shunted away from your skin, the thickness of the surface tissues is increased. In turn, the rate of your heat loss is greatly reduced.

Staying Warm During Cold-Weather Workouts

Cold weather usually does not present a significant problem for most individuals who desire to exercise outdoors. For instance, cold air does not pose a particular danger to your respiratory passages. By the time inspired cold air reaches your lungs, the air is warmed to a temperature level that is safe for respiratory tissue. In fact, healthy individuals can breathe air at temperatures as low as -31°F without any harmful or detrimental effects. Trust us on this one but don't try it!

Your ability to exercise will not be impaired provided that you maintain a relatively normal body temperature. This can be accomplished simply by wearing sufficient clothing to keep the surface areas of your body warm. Your maximal aerobic capacity and your oxygen cost of submaximal exercise are generally unaffected by the cold weather. Heart rate may be slightly lower during exercise in the cold, but this is not a consistent finding. Stroke volume (the amount of blood pumped by your heart per beat) tends to be higher at low exercise intensities but is not influenced by the cold weather at higher workloads. Cardiac output (the amount of blood pumped by the heart on a per minute basis) remains unchanged.

If your core temperature and muscle temperature fall below normal levels, your maximal aerobic capacity may be reduced. Cool muscles have a diminished ability to generate force for a given cross-sectional area of muscle fibers. In order to maintain an appropriate level of muscle force, more fast twitch (large) fibers must be recruited. The recruitment of fast twitch fibers results in a greater reliance on anaerobic glycolysis and, in turn, a greater production of lactic acid. As a result of this metabolic adjustment, your ability to perform activities that require dynamic muscular fitness can be adversely affected.

Fortunately, the process of maintaining your body's core temperature within normal levels and of insulating the exterior surface area of your body against the cold elements is not particularly difficult. As a matter of fact, your aerobic training efforts will enable your body to accomplish this heat regulation on a voluntary basis. During exercise, more than 75 percent of the energy produced by your working muscles is converted to heat, which elevates your core temperature. When your exercise intensity is moderate to high, you are able to generate a sufficient amount of heat to maintain your body's core temperature within normal ranges. At low intensities of exercise, however, your body's core temperature could start to fall after one hour of activity in the cold were it not for the onset of involuntary shivering thermogenesis.

As stated earlier, cold weather should not prevent you from exercising outdoors. You can safely exercise in the cold by simply following basic guidelines aimed at helping you make appropriate adjustments for the weather. Among the more common guidelines for ensuring that your exercise participation in the cold is, in fact, safe, are the following:

- Consult your physician. Before exercising in the cold, consult your physician if you have heart and/or lung disease. Breathing cold air is not in and of itself harmful to healthy people—cold air, as previously discussed, does not damage your lungs. It can, however, be risky for individuals who suffer from angina, asthma, or hypertension. At-risk individuals, if cleared by their physicians to exercise in the cold, should wear ski masks or scarves pulled loosely over their faces—this preventive act will help warm up inhaled air.

- Extend your warm-up period. Because it is often more difficult to warm up in the cold, it's a good idea to warm up and stretch indoors first and then stretch again outside before starting to exercise.

- Compensate for the wind. The wind can penetrate your clothing and eliminate the insulating layer of warm air around your body. You can compensate for a strong wind by running or riding against it on your way out, and then with it (behind you) on your way back. In this way, you will get the worst of the "wind chill factor" over with before you become too sweaty or tired.

- Drink plenty of fluids. It is relatively easy to become dehydrated in cold weather. You lose water from sweating and breathing since you have to warm and moisten the cold air you breathe. You also lose water because your urine output tends to be increased. As a result, you should drink fluids before, during, and after your workout. You should also avoid alcohol and caffeine—both of which can dehydrate you.

- Be alert. Shorter daylight hours, reduced visibility, and the risk of skidding cars require that you be particularly careful while running, walking, and cycling outdoors.

- Dress in layers. Wear several layers of loose-fitting, thin clothing. Such clothing will provide insulation and trap the heat you generate. You can also remove layers if you become too warm while exercising.

- Wear a waterproof, wind resistant but breathable, outer layer. It is important that your outer clothing not only provides you with protection from the elements (rain, snow, wind, etc.), but also allows your sweat to evaporate. Wet or damp clothing transfers heat away from your body approximately 20 times faster than dry clothing.

- Cover your head. Yes, mother knows best—large amounts of heat are lost from an uncovered head. A wool or synthetic cap is probably the best choice.

- Cover your hands. Wear gloves or mittens to protect your hands from the cold. In extreme cold, mittens are preferred over gloves since they keep your fingers together and have less surface area from which heat can escape.

- Wear good exercise shoes. Make sure that your shoes provide good traction and shock absorption—particularly if you run on hard, frozen ground.

- Wear socks made of absorbent, "breathable" material. Wear socks made of material that will trap warm air and keep your feet dry.

The key to exercising safely outdoors during times of inclement weather is to be prepared. Bundle up in layers. Unless the ambient temperature and wind say otherwise, don't let winter interfere with the benefits and joys of exercising out-of-doors.

EXERCISING AT HIGH ALTITUDE

Similar to hot and cold temperatures and air pollution, the relative altitude at which you exercise can have an effect on both your body and your performance level. The degree to which exercising at relatively high altitude affects your body ranges from basic physiological responses wrought by decreases in barometric pressure to an array of high altitude-related illnesses. Changes in your performance capabilities begin to manifest themselves at approximately 1,500 meters (5,000 feet).

How Your Body Reacts to Exercising at High Altitude

As you increase the altitude at which you are exercising, the barometric pressure decreases. Although the percentage of oxygen in the air stays fairly constant, as the altitude increases the amount of hemoglobin saturated with oxygen in your blood falls. Because the decrease in barometric pressure has a negative effect on the partial pressure of oxygen in the air you inhale, your level of hemoglobin saturation is also lowered. The net result is that since less oxygen is carried by your arterial blood, the amount of oxygen available at the cellular level is reduced. In turn, your level of maximal oxygen uptake (VO2max) and your physical working capacity (PWC) are reduced (relative to the increase in altitude). In an attempt to compensate for these changes, your body undergoes several adaptive responses. Submaximal heart rate, cardiac output, and pulmonary ventilation increase. To a point, your body can achieve the same level of submaximal performance, but has to work much harder physiologically to do so.

How Your Ability to Perform Is Affected at High Altitude

Your ability to perform physically tends to be affected once you reach an altitude of 5,000 feet. At that height (and beyond), your capacity to perform some tasks is enhanced, while your ability to do others is diminished. Those tasks which require your body to overcome resistance (e.g., sprinting, long jumping, etc.) are easier since the level of resistance is reduced concomitantly with the reduction in air density. On the other hand, those activities that have an aerobic component are much more difficult to perform. All factors considered, the more aerobic an activity is, the greater the negative effect that altitude has on performance. Because your blood contains less oxygen at higher altitudes, your heart has to beat more frequently to deliver a sufficient amount of oxygen to your working muscles. In other words, you have to work much harder to perform the same amount of aerobic work. As a result, you'll have to lower the intensity level of your exercise to keep within your prescribed training heart rate range.

High Altitude-Related Illnesses

Depending on the speed of ascent and the level of elevation you achieve, a number of illnesses can occur when you engage in physical activity at high altitude. These illnesses range in seriousness from relatively mild symptoms that resolve themselves with acclimatization to potentially fatal edema of your brain and lungs. Two of the more common conditions are acute mountain sickness and high altitude pulmonary edema.

Acute mountain sickness (AMS) is an altitude-related illness characterized by such symptoms as severe headache, nausea, vomiting, decreased appetite, weariness, and sleep disturbances. It is a relatively common condition among individuals who make a rapid ascent to altitudes to over 7,000 feet. The symptoms usually begin 4 to 6 hours after your ascent and often last 40 to 72 hours before they resolve themselves. In a rare few cases at higher altitudes, AMS may lead to more severe symptoms such as brain or lung edema. A rule of thumb to prevent AMS is to "rest" one day at 7,000 feet and another day for each additional 2,000 feet of increase in altitude. In addition, you should limit the extent and the speed of your ascent on any given day—depending on how severely AMS affects you.

High altitude pulmonary edema (HAPE) is a far more serious high altitude-related illness. This condition is characterized by leakage of fluid into the lungs. The fluid causes a shortness of breath, coughing, and a purple coloring (cyanosis) of the lips and extremities. The problems with breathing can rapidly progress to coma and death if they're not treated in an appropriate and immediate manner. The first step in the treatment process is to administer oxygen. The second (and often concurrent) step is to evacuate the victim to a lower altitude as soon as possible. Those individuals with HAPE who are evacuated tend to recover swiftly with few complications. Once you experience an episode of HAPE, you are at increased risk of developing it again when you return to high altitude. Consequently, you should strongly consider refraining from again engaging in vigorous exercise testing or training at high altitude.

Training at High Altitude

If you reside at a high altitude, it is probably unavoidable that you exercise at high altitude. Keep in mind, however, that if you travel to a high altitude in the belief that high altitude training will somehow benefit your ability to perform at sea level, you may be disappointed in the results of your efforts and may needlessly expose yourself to undue risk of high altitude illnesses. To date, the only unequivocal result that high altitude training has been shown to improve is your performance ability at that setting (i.e., if you train at 5,000 feet, your ability to perform at 5,000 feet is enhanced.)

EXERCISE AND AIR POLLUTION

The air in most major metropolitan areas is contaminated with a variety of gases and particulates that can have a detrimental effect on aerobic exercise performance. The severity of air pollution in a specific area is determined by a number of factors including the amount of pollutants produced in the area (e.g., automobile emissions, factories, etc.), meteorological phenomena (e.g., temperature inversions, low wind velocities, etc.), and geological conditions (e.g., cities located in basins or surrounded by mountains.) The major air pollutants are carbon monoxide, ozone, and sulfur oxides. During times of temperature inversion, or when the air becomes stagnant, the level of these major air pollutants can reach concentrations that severely impair your aerobic performance capability. The increased depth and rate of breathing associated with relatively intense aerobic exercise exacerbate the impact of polluted air on you because the rate at which the pollutants are absorbed by your respiratory system is increased.

The Big Three Pollutants

- Carbon Monoxide. Carbon monoxide is an odorless gas which limits the ability of your blood to transport oxygen. It is the most common pollutant. The primary sources of carbon monoxide are cigarette smoke and automobile exhaust emissions. Regardless of its origin, carbon monoxide causes problems because of its strong affinity for binding to the hemoglobin molecules of red blood cells. Carbon monoxide has an affinity for hemoglobin which is approximately 210 times greater than that of oxygen. Thus, whenever a molecule of carbon monoxide and a molecule of oxygen compete for the same hemoglobin attachment site, the carbon monoxide molecule always wins. As a result, less oxygen is transported per unit volume of blood and provided to the myoglobin of the muscle cells by the red blood cells. Consequently, your heart is required to work harder and beat more frequently to compensate for the less-than-adequate concentration of oxygen in your blood. Eventually, the net results of the oxygen deficit and your heart's efforts to compensate are a decrease in maximum oxygen uptake (VO2max) and physical work capacity. Once your blood concentration of carbon monoxide reaches a critical level (3% or greater), exercise performance—both submaximal and maximal— will be significantly diminished.

- Ozone. Ozone is a pollutant that is produced by the action of sunlight on the hydrocarbons and nitrogen dioxide in the air. Of all the pollutants found in significant amounts in urban areas, ozone is generally regarded as the most toxic and causes the largest decrements in aerobic performance. The potential effects of ozone depend upon the duration of your exposure to ozone (e.g., short-term or long-term) and the level of ozone concentration in the atmosphere. Among the effects of short-term exposure to high concentrations of ozone are eye irritation and an increased level of airway resistance. The increased level of resistance causes an increase in the rate and a decrease in the depth of your breathing. As a result, the level of maximum ventilation during exercise is decreased, the energy cost of breathing is increased, and your aerobic capacity is temporarily diminished. Long-term exposure to high levels of ozone, on the other hand, has negative health implications, such as obstruction of your respiratory bronchioles and nausea. If you have asthma or allergies, you should avoid exercising in high ozone areas. Chest tightness, coughing, wheezing, shortness of breath, headaches, etc. — all common symptoms after inhaling ozone — can last up to 24 hours after the completion of an exercise bout in a high ozone environment.

- Sulfur Oxides. Primarily in the form of sulfur dioxides, sulfur oxide pollutants come from the combustion of sulfur-containing fossil fuels. When inhaled, sulfur oxides dissolve quickly in the moisture coating the mucous membranes of your lungs, and irritate your upper respiratory tract. This irritation frequently brings about reflex bronchoconstriction (i.e., a narrowing of the air passages in your lungs — a process which inhibits the flow of oxygen to and from your lungs) and an increased level of airway resistance. Similar to the effects of ozone, overexposure to sulfur oxides often causes you to cough and wheeze when exercising.

The Effects of Air Pollution

A by-product of extremely complex chemical reactions, air pollution can negatively impact your aerobic exercise capacity in several ways. The magnitude of air pollution's effect is at least partly related to the ability of pollutants (e.g., carbon monoxide, ozone, sulfur dioxide, etc.) to infiltrate your respiratory system.

When you are not exercising, your respiratory tract serves as both the major route of infiltration for air pollutants and the major barrier to their penetration. For example, during normal breathing, the mucous membranes in your nose are very effective in removing large particulate matter and highly soluble gases from the air that reaches your lungs. On the other hand, during aerobic exercise you tend to breathe through your mouth. In turn, the natural air filtration process of your body becomes less efficient, resulting in more pollutants reaching your lungs. Once in the lungs, many of these pollutants subsequently diffuse into your bloodstream and circulate through your body.

Since your respiratory tract is the largest surface area of your body to come in contact with air pollutants, many of the adverse effects of air pollution occur in that region. Among the many negative physiological effects of air pollution are the following:

- Bronchial vasoconstriction (i.e., the airway openings in your lungs become smaller), which results in increased airway resistance.
- Your lungs lose some of their diffusing surface area either as a result of destruction of the alveoli (i.e., the functional units of the lung) or as a by-product of an increased level of mucus secretion.
- Your oxygen transport capacity is reduced. Less oxygen enters your bloodstream (via the pulmonary system), resulting in an inadequate supply of oxygenated blood to your working (i.e., exercising) muscles.

Exercise Precautions

- You can control or at least minimize the potential effect of exercising in high pollution areas by taking the following steps:
- Avoid exercising outdoors when smog (air pollution) alerts have been issued. Pollution Standard Index (PSI) readings exceeding 100 are considered unhealthy.

- Avoid exercising outdoors in urban areas where heavy traffic exists during times when air pollutants are at their highest levels (e.g., 7-10 a.m. and 4-7 p.m.).

- Avoid exercising outdoors when the ambient temperature and the humidity levels are high.

- Avoid exercising during hours when the sun is brightest (since research shows that ozone levels increase on sunny days).

- Exercise as much as possible in open areas — where air currents can move freely, thereby dispersing any pollutants in the air.

- Reduce your exercise intensity level and duration when pollution levels are high or when your breathing becomes labored or impaired.

- Avoid secondhand cigarette smoke before, during, and after exercise.

- When pollution levels are unacceptable, exercise indoors.

A Breath of Fresh Air

The basic approach you should take when dealing with the potentially adverse effects of air pollution on your aerobic exercise performance is relatively straightforward—avoid exercising in locations where or at times when air pollution levels are unacceptably high. Breathing clean air is usually taken for granted by almost everyone. Clean air, however, plays a critical role in keeping your lungs "clean" and functioning properly. The benefits of aerobic exercise are numerous and well documented. In order to maximize your ability to attain those benefits, you need to exercise in environments that are user-friendly to your lungs (i.e., relatively pollution–free environments). Environments in which you can breathe a breath of fresh air.

About the Authors

Jason Conviser is President of JMC & Associates and is one of the nation's experts in articulating the opportunity where the traditional health care continuum and health care services are expanded and offered in the health club setting. Throughout his career, he has lectured and written about the relationship between the exercise and health. Dr. Conviser holds a Ph.D. from the University of Wisconsin-Madison, an MBA from Northwestern University, and is a Fellow of the American College of Sports Medicine.

Jenny Conviser is a psychologist who specializes in eating disorders, sport psychology, and women's issues. Dr. Conviser is an Assistant Professor of Psychology in the Medical School of Northwestern University and is on the staff of Northwestern Memorial Hospital. She holds a Psy.D. from the Chicago School of Professional Psychology, and a masters degree in exercise physiology from Northern Illinois University, and has completed an internship in the behavioral medicine program of the University of Chicago Hospitals. Dr. Conviser is also a Certified Sport Psychologist.

Greg Ewert is a board certified specialist in both internal medicine and sport medicine. Dr. Ewert is on staff of Northwestern Memorial Hospital and a partner with Michigan Avenue Internists in Chicago. He is the medical director of the Chicago Marathon and one of the team physicians for the Chicago Blackhawk's, and medical consultant to the Chicago Bears. Dr. Ewert earned his medical degree at the University of Illinois College of Medicine. He completed medical training at Northwestern University Feinberg School of Medicine. Dr. Ewert is a member of the You Turn Sport Medicine Advisory Board.